THE ART OF
CARTOONING

THE ART OF
CARTOONING

Syd Hoff

STRAVON EDUCATIONAL PRESS
New York

Previously copyrighted material appearing
in this book is reprinted by permission.
Some of the material in this book originally appeared under
the title *Learning to Cartoon* by Syd Hoff, copyright © 1966
by Stravon Educational Press, which *The Art of Cartooning* replaces.

Library of Congress Cataloging in Publication Data

Hoff, Sydney, 1912–
    The art of cartooning.

    1.   Caricature.   I.   Title.
NC1320.H53   741.5'973   72–12659
ISBN 0–87396–072–6

Manufactured in the United States of America

CONTENTS

Dedication

Perhaps millions of years ago some Paleolithic creature one day wandered into a cave with conventional art on the walls, laid down his club, and blacked in a tooth or drew in a mustache. This seems possible because Man certainly could have used a laugh in those dim, distant days.

Until that particular cave is found and the fact established, then, I'd like to dedicate this book to that unknown creature—the father of all cartoonists.

Cartooning is fine art with a sense of humor.
—AL CAPP

PREFACE

It's embarrassing to find myself in the position of "teacher," when I continue to think of myself as more of a *student* of cartooning after these many years of selling my work to magazines and newspapers. Yet that is precisely the feeling of most of my fellow-professionals—we never stop learning.

For just as we were affected by our contemporaries and predecessors when *we* were beginners, we continue to learn something every day from the talented newcomers making their debut in the various media. It is the cycle of life. We learn from them, they learn from us.

There is no shame in this. "No man is an island, entire of itself," as the philosopher John Donne said. The flowering of genius in any individual's art is really the culmination of the efforts of many. The dancer learned from other dancers. The composer learned from other composers. To go to another extreme, if a person is learning how to hit a baseball, he would be silly not to try to glean something from Hank Aaron or Harmon Killebrew, wouldn't he?

And that is the purpose of this book: to set down before the reader a sampling of the very best work of cartoonists—some old, some new— so that each can examine the work of the other and benefit accordingly. For the novice, I have included as clear and comprehensive a course in cartooning as possible, I believe, from faces to figures to composition— and finally an explanation of how to think up ideas for the kind of drawings seen in most publications and prepare them for market. The casual

"Are you sticking out your tongue at me?"

"Then there was the time I broke my glasses."

"Relax, dear, it's Flossie's birthday."

student, I feel, will at least have a good time perusing all this and even learn how to make funny pictures. The more serious student, the one who decides to stick to the profession and try to make it his livelihood, will at least be apprised of some of the pitfalls.

Cartooning is a happy art. It is indeed, as Mr. Capp says, "fine art with a sense of humor." Enjoy this book for whatever you hoped to get out of it, and please join me in thanking my colleagues without whom all this would have been possible, but not very probable, in the following alphabetical order:

Alfred Andriola, Jose Aruego, Frank Asch, Tony Auth, Robert Baldwin (Rupe), Martin Banner, Gene Basset, C. D. Batchelor, Jeanne Bendick, Bud Blake, Herbert L. Block (Herblock), Henry Boltinoff, Wayne Boring, Buck Brown, David Brown, Marcia Brown, Dik Browne, Ernie Bushmiller, Milton Caniff, Al Capp, John Celardo, Jacqueline Chwast, George Clark, Roy Crane, Charlie Daniel, Tom Darcy, Whitney Darrow Jr., Robert Day, Eldon Dedini, Tony DeLuna, John Dirks, Rudy Dirks, Walt Disney, Don Dowling, Bob Dunn, Roger Duvoisin, Tom Engelhardt, Gioia Fiammenghi, John Fischetti, Bud Fisher, James Flora, Paul Galdone, Ted Geisel (Dr. Seuss), Carl Giles, Chester Gould, John Groth, Eric and Nancy Gurney, Garry Clark Hamilton, Harry Hanan, Hanna-Barbera, Jimmy Hatlo, George Herriman, Erwin Hess, Ned Hilton, Al Hirschfeld, Phil Interlandi, Jim Ivey, Ferd Johnson, Larry Katzman (Kaz), Al Kaufman, Bil Keane, Reamer

Keller, Steven Kellogg, Jack Kent, Warren King, Fernando Krahn, Robert Kraus, Jim Lange, Fred Lasswell, Mell Lazarus, Lank Leonard, Guernsey LePelley, Robert Leydenfrost, Marty Links, Ranan Lurie, Don Madden, Jerry Marcus, Doug Marlette, Bill Mauldin, Dale Messik, Henning Dahl Mikkelsen, Frank Modell, Zack Mosley, Ken Muse, Fred Neher, Ed Nofziger, Pat Oliphant, Virgil Partch (Vip), Susan Perl, Roy Peterson, Carl Pfeufer, George Price, Gardner Rea, Ed Reed, Mischa Richter, Mitchell Rose, Al Ross, Bud Sagendorf, Bill Sanders, Charles Saxon, Alvaro Scaduto, Charles M. Schulz, Elzie Segar, Ted Shearer, Charles E. Slackman, Al Smith, Mr. and ·Mrs. George Smith, Mark Alan Stamaty, William Steig, Paul Szep, Jack Tippit, Barney Tobey, Wallace Tripp, Morrie Turner, Max Van Bibber, Raeburn Van Buren, Mort Walker, L. D. Warren, M. S. Weiss, Gahan Wilson, Bernard Wiseman, Don Wright, Chic Young—as well as numerous editors, syndicates, newspapers, and advertising agencies.

"By an odd coincidence, that's how many errors he made last year."

1. FACES

Oscar Wilde said it about certain characteristic British faces, that "once seen they are never remembered." Be that as it may, the famous poet, playwright, and wit had no choice but to go on looking at faces anyway—and neither do we. So, let us begin our study of cartooning by drawing a face. Does that frighten you? All right, then we'll draw something easier instead—a bagel.

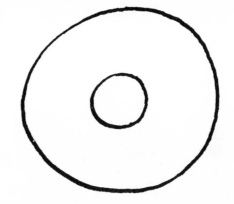

(If you don't know how to draw a bagel, draw a doughnut.)

All that remains now is to add the eyes and mouth.

Wasn't that simple so far?

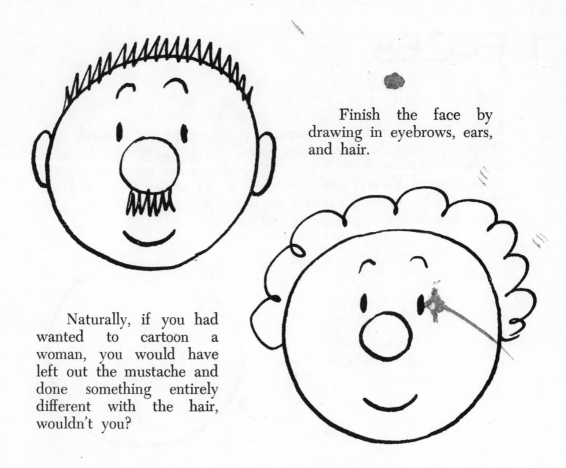

Finish the face by drawing in eyebrows, ears, and hair.

Naturally, if you had wanted to cartoon a woman, you would have left out the mustache and done something entirely different with the hair, wouldn't you?

All right, so you're not ready yet to start selling to major markets. What do you expect from a mere bagel?

"How do I plead? *This* is how I plead!"

The horrifying thought occurs to me that since you are studying the "Hoff method" of cartooning, you might end up by drawing like me—although I once took a Fred Astaire course in dancing, and still have two left feet. Therefore, as an antidote, here are cartoons from three very popular newspaper features.

THE FAMILY CIRCUS   **By Bil Keane**

"Could I get a new bike? The one I got for Christmas went out of style."

© 1972 Register & Tribune Syndicate

THE LITTLE WOMAN

"You want to go back and try again? You missed one."

© 1972 King Features Syndicate, Inc.

OFF THE RECORD   **By Ed Reed**

BOB + DORIS

"Bob, how long will we have to economize before we can afford inflation?"

© 1972 Register & Tribune Syndicate

Notice how these famous cartoonists handle the problem of faces!

Ready now for a side view, or profile? For this we won't need the bagel any more. We'll use an egg and an orange. (It makes no difference if the egg is medium or hard-boiled.)

1. Egg and orange touching each other.

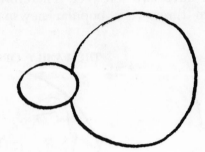

2. Same objects with eye and mouth added.

3. Finished profile with ear, mustache, hair, and eyebrow.

4. Female of the species. Oops! We forgot to leave out the mustache!

Another drawing of mine, this time from *Esquire Magazine*.
You can almost see the egg on Papa's face, can't you? As for Mama, doesn't she resemble a bagel?

"Please, John, don't ruin a wonderful evening!"

Despite the war on poverty, alas, there are still some homes where there are no bagels, eggs, or oranges. Hence, plain squares will have to be used in making a face.

1. Make a square.

2. Divide it thusly.

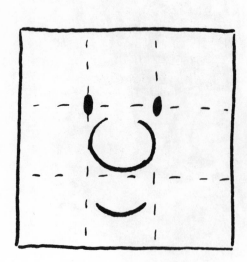

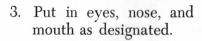

3. Put in eyes, nose, and mouth as designated.

4. *Voila!*

Profiles can be made the same way.

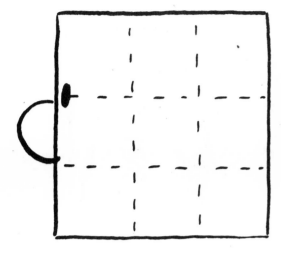 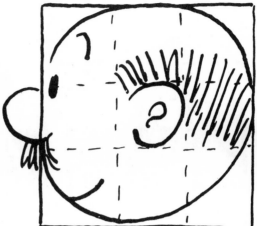

1. Notice the nose extends outside the square.

2. Fill in the features as designated.

The faces in this cartoon by Henry Boltinoff are worthy of close scrutiny—even the dog's!

"He's our base runner!"

Now notice you don't have to deal in "squares" at all! Make an assortment of odd shapes and try to make faces out of them!

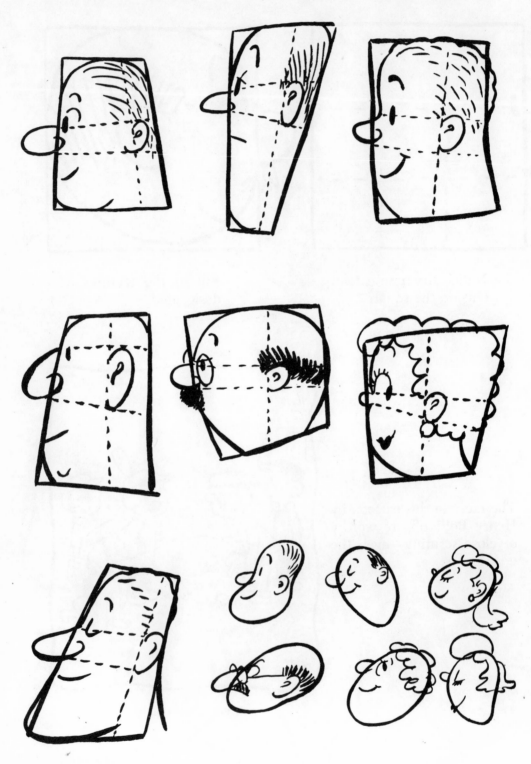

In this cartoon I capitalized on the fact that some people are eggheads.

"Oh, yes—and a dozen eggs."

However, don't blame hens for the shape the rest of us are in.

These are faces created by the late cartoonist Lank Leonard for his great comic strip "Mickey Finn."

MICKEY FINN

MRS. FINN

CLANCY

SHERIFF PHILIP FINN

Observe how the basic structure of all these faces is the bagel. Take "Uncle Phil" (Sheriff Finn), for instance.

Get it?

TOM COLLINS

MICKEY FINN   **LANK LEONARD**

NOWHERE DID ANY-ONE SELL A BOAT FOR CASH!

ONE PLACE DID! BUT THE MAN SAID IT WASN'T DRAYNE —AND IT'S BEEN **BOTHERIN'** ME!

3-20

FRED—SUPPOSE DRAYNE CUT OFF HIS MUSTACHE, GOT RID OF HIS SIDEBURNS —HE COULD BE WEARIN' A TOUPEE—OR HE MIGHT HAVE DYED HIS HAIR!

WE'LL HAVE AN ARTIST DRAW HIM WITHOUT THE MUSTACHE—AND WITH LIGHT HAIR —AND SEE IF THE MAN IDENTIFIES HIM!

I **KNOW** THAT GIRL!

These familiar children's faces (and Snoopy's) are from Charles M. Schulz' award-winning comic strip "Peanuts," about which we'll read more later.

PATTY

SHERMY

VIOLET

CHARLIE BROWN

PIG-PEN

SALLY BROWN

SCHROEDER

SNOOPY

LUCY

LINUS

FRIEDA

A FACE CAN BE MADE OUT OF ANY LETTER IN THE ALPHABET. (The Phoenician alphabet, anyway.)

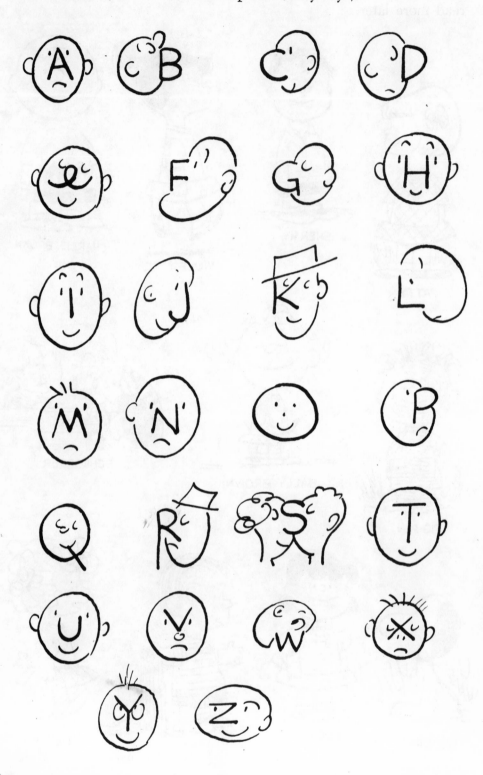

The same applies to numbers.

What city does this spell out?

Study the comic-strip and magazine cartoonists.

Practice improvising faces out of numbers and letters. Study the faces of men and women all around you. Be careful when you're studying women. I once knew a fellow. . . .

EASY CARTOONS

Man With Fly On Nose

Stout Woman Leaning Out Window

Cross-eyed Man Looking Around Corner

Man With Disgust Written All Over His Face

Infant Crying

Same Infant a Month Later

Ain't Cartooning Fun?

2. EXPRESSIONS

"Who, me?"

It may sound funny or farfetched but cartoonists can learn something about facial expressions from the Old Masters. For instance, in their portraits, Italians like Leonardo and Michelangelo run the whole gamut from agony to ecstasy, Spaniards like Velasquez teach us to strive for a penetration of personality, while Franz Hals and Rembrandt of the Dutch school imbue us with a feeling of joy and warmth.

So, young cartoonist, get thee to a museum and see how all of the above, as well as Cezanne, Renoir, Matisse, Picasso, and many others, handled faces. Take along your pad and pencil. You may want to make notes of what they did with eyes and mouths and chins. And if the guard should peek over your shoulder and sneer, don't let it go to waste. Make a sketch of his expression too!

In this cartoon I tried to concentrate on the expression of the girl on the left.

"Things aren't working out the way I expected. He likes my cooking and we never go out to eat."

27

The two most commonly known expressions in cartoondom are GLAD and MAD. Here they are:

GLAD

MAD

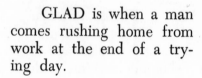

GLAD is when a man comes rushing home from work at the end of a trying day.

MAD is when his wife tells him they're eating out again, or that she just bought a new hat.

You will note that practically the only thing remaining unchanged on the man was his hat. In *GLAD* his eyebrows and mouth were turned up. In *MAD*—well, it shouldn't happen to a dog.

An excellent study of facial expressions is found in Ferd Johnson's earthy, mirthy strip "Moon Mullins."

Moon Mullins   **by Ferd Johnson**

EYES

Let us examine closely some of the features that determine expression.

Just two
black spots
will do

You can
roll 'em

Stare with
'em

Close 'em

Look sleepy
with 'em

Wink 'em

Get a shiner
with 'em

Weep with
'em

Or maybe you'd
rather get drunk
or K.O.'d

Eyes, sayeth the poet, are the keys to the soul. The cartoonist also thinks they're important—so study these!

NOSES

Pugnacious

Aristocratic

Button

Cop's

Itsy Bitsy

Hawk

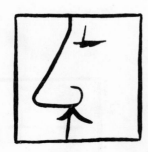

Roman

Alcoholic

Mine

Sometimes it's worth
holding on to these things.

MOUTHS

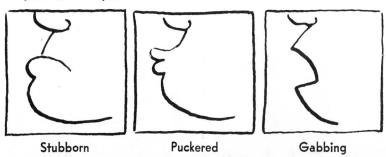

Stubborn   Puckered   Gabbing

CHINS

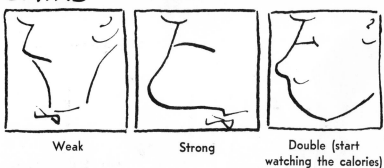

Weak   Strong   Double (start watching the calories)

HAIR (women)

Mama   Daughter   Aunt Prunella

HAIR (men)

What I once had   Going—going—   —gone!

Mother has a sweet expression on her face in this cartoon, but do you think it's sweet enough to talk the cop out of that ticket?

"Do you prefer police work to Hollywood, Mr. Peck?"

INKidentally, did you ever notice the different kinds of glasses people wear?

Small Businessman

Legislator

Dowager

Big Businessman

Fop

I can never find mine!

Harry Hanan's "Louie" never says a word. He doesn't have to because his facial expressions are funny enough, as you can see by this Sunday page.

It's very simple to escalate expressions.

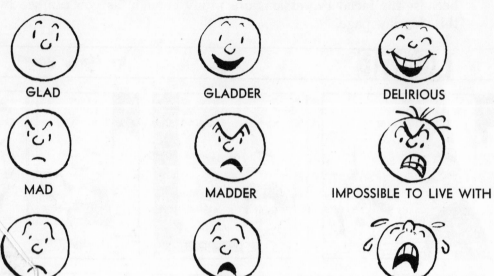

GLAD   GLADDER   DELIRIOUS

MAD   MADDER   IMPOSSIBLE TO LIVE WITH

SAD   SADDER   REALLY, NOW!

GEOGRAPHY LESSON

The—   —human—   —map—   —keeps—

—changing—   —all—   —the—   time!

IMPORTANT!

As a cartoonist it is wise to remember that overdoing expressions may sometimes ruin a cartoon, or change its entire meaning. (The same is true in reverse—"*under-doing*" an expression.)

For example, let us say that you have an occasion to draw a hospital scene in which the doctor has come out of a patient's room and is saying to the waiting wife, "Your husband's much better, ma'am—he's pinching all the nurses." Obviously, if the doctor is screaming those words in a rage, or has a melancholy look on his face like Hamlet, he will kill the drawing—if he hasn't already killed the patient. Your doctor should simply have his mouth open in a normal conversation lest the idea take on some remote interpretation.

By the same token if you are drawing a child in a police station saying to the desk sergeant, "I'm lost. What flavor ice cream do you have today?"—it would be wrong to have the child thin, gaunt, and hungry-looking. The intelligent cartoonist would simply draw an average, well-fed brat to whom the ice cream or whole stale gag didn't really mean a thing.

This is not to say that there aren't times when we *must* use expressions that convey extreme emotional duress. Take a situation in a dentist's office to illustrate the point. The dentist is holding a drill in his hand and says to the frightened patient, "Now, this won't hurt a bit." Unless that dentist suddenly looks like a werewolf to his patient, the gag won't mean a thing.

Finally, let's say you are showing a pretty young thing in the dead of winter arriving at the corner of Fifth and Main where her boy friend has been standing. "Waiting long?" she asks. You won't get a laugh unless the b.f. looks frozen stiff, like he's been hung up at the North Pole for at least a month.

"I'm only allo..ed one call, Marge. Now what was that you wanted to tell me about Edith?"

An example of good and bad expressions.

GOOD

1.

"I'd climb the highest mountain and swim the deepest river, just to get away from you!"

BAD

2.

"I'd climb the highest mountain and swim the deepest river, just to get away from you!"

No. 2 is bad because Mama shouldn't react in a pleased way to a crack like that. She should either look hurt as I have her in No. 1, or angry. Also, this is definitely not the kind of remark Dad would make in a quiet, refined way. More likely he'd be in a temper brought on perhaps by the sight of still another frozen TV dinner on the stove, or news that his mother-in-law is arriving for a six months stay.

Another example of good and bad expressions.

GOOD

"You don't need lessons. You
need a kick in the pants."

BAD

"You don't need lessons.
You need a kick in the pants."

No. 2 is all wrong, of course, because that kid should be squirm-
ing to get away from the piano and back to stickball or hockey. And
his teacher shouldn't look like he can stand much more torture,
either.

*Figure out what makes your characters tick before deciding how
to draw them! Don't let your cartoons become like oldtime movies
where "overacting" often spoiled them!*

Great expressions are achieved by prolific Al Kaufman in these two cartoons.

Observe Mother so blasé, the kids just munching away, and poor Dad wondering if he'll ever get credit for doing *anything* right!

"Do you realize how long it's been since we've eaten in?"

© Look

This one by Kaufman needed no caption—the expressions were enough. The lady with the umbrella, so dainty and demure, gazes askance at the little guy having himself a ball lapping up all that water.

© The Saturday Evening Post

I tried to tell the whole story with my faces in this cartoon:

"Actually, I am a success. In school, I was voted least likely to succeed."

Count how many different expressions Jack Tippitt has drawn
in these panels from his popular newspaper feature "Amy."

AMY By Jack Tippit

"No, my mother isn't home, but I'll take a message if you'll talk slowly and spell all the words."

AMY By Jack Tippit

"Roger just gave me two salamanders . . . should I keep them or hurt his feelings?"

AMY By Jack Tippit

"If they look a little sick, it's because I painted them when I had a virus."

AMY By Jack Tippit

"I hope you don't mind competition . . . I'M planning to be a teacher when I grow up."

"How else can I describe it to Norma?"

"Do you mind, Mr. Miller? . . . It's the first
letter I ever typed without making a mistake!"

"What would I like to hear?
The front door closing behind HIM!"

"I'll go along with you . . .
if you've got the nerve to wear it!"

Indiana-born Fred Ne-
her has been doing the
syndicated panel "Life's
Like That" for thirty years.
He also teaches a course in
cartooning at the University
of Colorado—so, pay attention!

"Mom just brought law and order
to this part of the West!"

"Hurry . . . here comes the nurse!"

"If Jimmy is such a lover of music,
why doesn't he get a
record player of his own?"

"Nonsense!" © Look

The opposing clergymen's faces in this Eldon Dedini cartoon had to be just right—one wise and smug, the other fierce and contradictory.

Study Dedini's faces in this picture, then copy them. He won't mind. (You can even sell the cartoon again, as long as you turn over the money to him!)

Study your own face—if you can stand it. Make cartoons of everybody you know. Only, for heaven's sake, don't show them! I've lost more friends that way. . . .

Here are a few more expressions:

Lovesick   Shy   Seasick   Z-z-zzzz

Suspicious   Hic!   Ah—choo!   Oops, must be that stuffed cabbage

That's about all I, and my confreres, can tell you about faces at this time. It's true there are other types—some people are two-faced, some have faces only a mother could love, some have faces that could stop a clock. If any of these feel slighted because they were omitted, I'll just have to *face* the music.

Keep practicing everything we've done so far. See who can create the biggest pile of scrap paper in your house. Copy. Trace. Then do it all by memory. Get everything down pat, as Mike said.

And speaking of expressions, there is still one more: "I'll be seeing you." In the next chapter, I mean.

"'M' is for the million things she gave us, 'O' is for . . ."

In George Price's hand a drawing pen becomes naturally biting and satiric, and the human race becomes the human *comedy*. These faces show you why he is known as "the cartoonist's cartoonist."

3. FIGURES

Three spots
by Ted
Shearer.

Mention the word "figure" to the average man and he'll either start thinking of the opposite sex or his income tax. The young cartoonist endeavoring to shape his career is, of course, not yet concerned with the latter—not as much as he'd like to be anyway. He has learned to draw faces and expressions, if he's been following this book, and now he'd like to place them on bodies that look proportionate, animate, and funny—all at the same time. How should he go about doing this?

Ever since ancient times Man has been extolling his own body in painting and sculpture—indeed, in all the arts. The cartoonist joins in this narcissism wholeheartedly. After all, the human form is a thing of infinite grace and beauty—perhaps more so than any other living thing in the universe.

ABBIE an' SLATS®

By Raeburn Van Buren

Former magazine illustrator Raeburn Van Buren's "Abbie an' Slats" comic strip is naturally replete with superb figure drawing and colorful characterizations.

Martin Branner's "Winnie Winkle" has kept her svelte figure almost forty years, and she was in her twenties when the strip started!

Winnie Winkle

The cartoonist may be only a comic impressionist but he too feels both a challenge and a responsibility to capture this grace and beauty. He, just as the painter and sculptor, longs to create figures that can stand, walk, run, jump, dance, and go through the rest of the motions as though they are imbued with life itself. Even if he has only a "slapstick" style, he knows the importance of achieving *good drawing*.

Why must a cartoon have "good drawing?" Because it is a one—two message. One, the reader looks—two, he laughs. In comic art, if a reader has to stop and puzzle over an inept drawing, the rhythm is broken and no matter how funny the idea is, the chances of him laughing at it are considerably lessened.

Larry Katzman ("Kaz") has a good figure under wraps on the left, and on the right his "Nellie Nifty, R.N." gives us an anatomy lesson of her own.

© Modern Medicine

"I think daddy's going to be mad when he wakes up."

Come to think of it, some of my own gals are pretty sexy too, wouldn't you say? This was a spoof of the *Esquire* calendar girl.

(My fine art instructors at the National Academy of Design forgave me these drawings. Robert Frost never forgave me the poetry.)

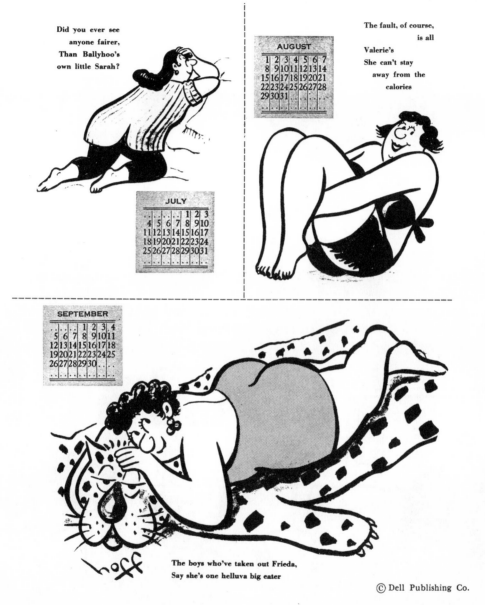

Did you ever see
anyone fairer,
Than Ballyhoo's
own little Sarah?

JULY

The fault, of course,
is all
Valerie's
She can't stay
away from the
calories

AUGUST

SEPTEMBER

The boys who've taken out Frieda,
Say she's one helluva big eater

The great Leonardo da Vinci learned his anatomy by spending long years in dissection, like a surgeon, clamping back skin and tissue in order to inspect the bones and muscles beneath the surface of the human body. In fact, some of Leonardo's drawings on the subject are still widely used to this day in authoritative medical journals.

But, hold on! Just because Leonardo da Vinci made like a ghoul I wasn't suggesting you hot foot it over to the nearest cemetery and dig yourself up a cadaver. That's not necessary at all. What I do recommend is that you simply take note of a few basic characteristics of the human form that you may have overlooked on your last trip to the beach, or vacation at a nudist camp.

It would be lovely if you could start right out drawing figures like Raeburn Van Buren, Reamer Keller, or Martin Branner, but unfortunately there are no short cuts in this business. You'll have to start out as they did, at the beginning. And in the beginning, as everybody knows, there were a couple of people named Adam and Eve, both of whom dressed pretty much alike.

How were these two people constructed, and everyone else who's come along since?

Two cartoons by Reamer Keller illustrate the "zip" for which he is famous.

"His troop got lost and was found by a troop of Girl Scouts."

"I became a secretary because I didn't want to do housework!"

Sitting, standing, or just being plain beguiling, famed theatrical caricaturist Al Hirschfeld inevitably achieves perfect figure drawing, plus uncanny likenesses, as demonstrated in this study of (left to right) Shelly Berman, Bert Lahr, and Nancy Walker, appearing on Broadway in *The Girls Against the Boys*.

From *The American Theatre of Al Hirschfeld*, published by George Braziller

BASIC PROPORTIONS

The human body is divided into four parts. (This does not apply to midgets who sometimes have only one or two, or basketball players who often achieve as much as eight or ten.)

FRONT VIEW

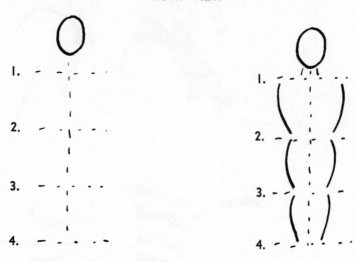

1. Top section includes both head and neck.

2. Sketch three curved lines tapered down gradually to ankles.

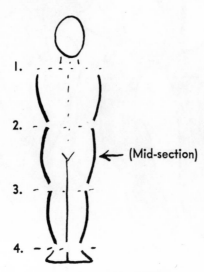

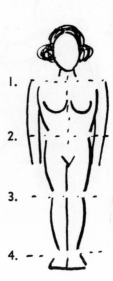

3. Add feet below fourth section

4. Sketch in arms.

REAR AND SIDE VIEW

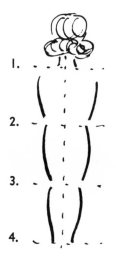

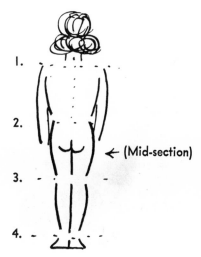

← (Mid-section)

1. Sketch curved lines tapering to ankles.

2. Note buttocks halfway between sections two and three.

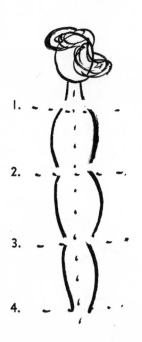

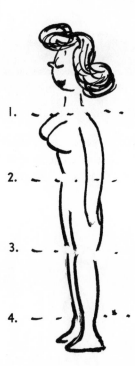

The Creator used a better blueprint than this (thank God!), but for cartoonistic purposes, our version should suffice. If you need additional reference, perhaps the lady across the street won't draw her blind tonight.

According to Michelangelo, the human body is beautiful "not only because of its form but because of its spiritual and ethical significance, the state of mind or soul its form could so successfully express."

We cartoonists go along with that not only because it's true but because, after all, who are we to argue with Michelangelo? And like the master who drew countless sketches of models in the nude before he painted them in clothing, we too try to know what "lies underneath" before we make a finished drawing.

© 1965 King Features Syndicate, Inc.

This little sketch of cartoonist Fred Lasswell's wouldn't have seemed nearly so funny if he hadn't let us "see" Snuffy Smith's body under that sheet.

Similarly, if I wanted to draw a lady in a dress, I would do it in two steps.

And if I wanted to make a man bowing politely, I would do it the same way.

This is a finished drawing of mine—

"For me it will end today if you don't say yes, Louise."

—and here is the preliminary sketch I made for the same picture.

Do you think I should have sold the sketch, instead?

Another preliminary sketch—

—and the finished draw-
ing it became!

© 1962
The New Yorker Magazine, Inc.

"But, gee, Muriel! <u>Somebody</u> has to marry stockboys!"

Have a good idea of what your figures look like before you do them!

Gardner Rea turned out laughs for over forty years, but dodged the whole problem of drawing a figure in this cartoon.

"Then one day when I was only six, a psychoanalyst's ceiling suddenly crashed down and hit me on the head!"

© 1000 Jokes

Two more by the great Rea.

"Heads, I won, Hartley! We name it after you."

© Saturday Review

© 1946 The New Yorker Magazine, Inc.

"Albert, how big a standing army do you suppose we'd have to have to stay at peace with the whole world?"

My young man is trying hard to imagine a figure in this drawing.

"She's still in the shower. Want to run your fingers through her hair while you wait?"

Cartoon by Hoff
Reprinted from LOOK Magazine, 1968

The hubby in Reamer Keller's drawing is trying to imagine one, too!

"Must you go out tonight, John? Please don't leave me alone with the refrigerator!"

Al Kaufman provides us with a cute figure study as well as a smashing gag in this six-panel cartoon.

TOO MANY MIRRORS

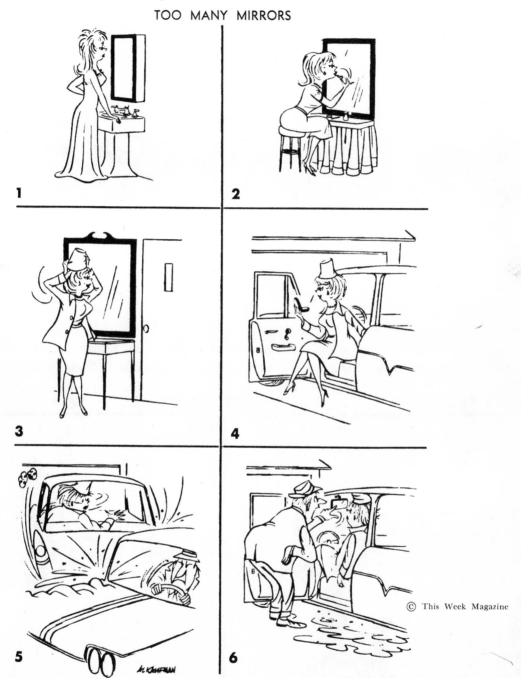

"Don't you ever look in the mirror, lady?"

Figure-shmigure! Kaufman's moral here might be, "Watch where you're driving!"

John Celardo illustrates the importance of good drawing in this single figure from his strip "Tarzan."

In "Emma Lou," famous female cartoonist Marty Links deliberately makes her adolescents extra-long to accentuate their gawkiness.

EMMY LOU®

By Marty Links

"Just by way of opening the conversation — are you going steady?"

"I'm not bothered by my break-up with Alvin, but I don't think this sympathy card was necessary!"

George Clark's panel "The Neighbors" is a daily art class, even for *professional* cartoonists!

Clark can afford to be "loose and sketchy." He knows what to put in and what to leave out.

"Happy birthday to me . . . happy birthday to me . . . happy birthday, dear Mommie . . . happy birthday to me."

"It's supposed to say 'peace is good, war is bad' but somehow it looks more like the beginning of World War III."

Thus far in this chapter you've been admiring some pretty nifty cartoon figures, kids, and if you're like me you're eating your heart out with jealousy. "How can I make my figures like some of those guys?" you're asking.

A tried and true way is to use "matchstick" figures as a springboard. If you've stopped smoking, don't let it worry you. Toothpicks will serve the purpose just as well. Get yourself about a dozen of these and lay them down on your pad, constructing a skeleton figure, thusly:

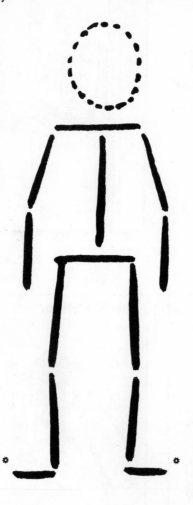

Sketch in an oval-shaped head.

* (Note that these sticks are half the size of the others.)

Here we have a perfectly good skeleton and we didn't have to disturb anyone's rest.

Hold the pieces and trace them on your pad. Save the tracing for future reference. Now you are ready to rearrange the sticks in other positions.

Some more skeletons

DAGWOOD, MAN OF ACTION!

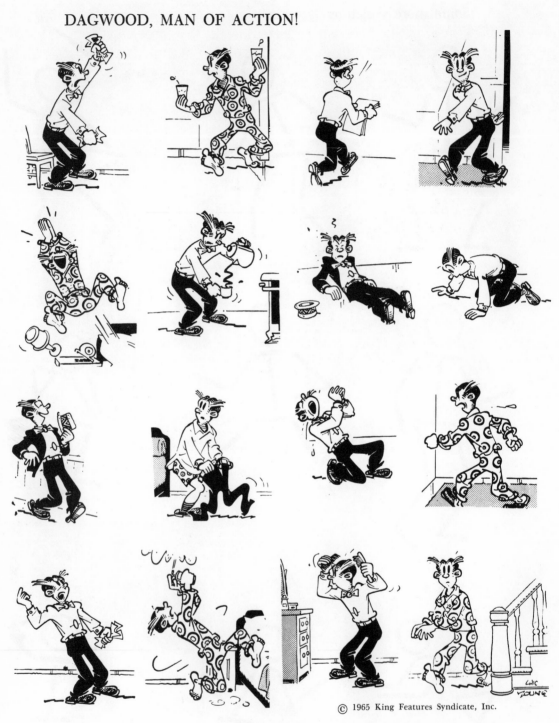

Whether it's his boss Mr. Dithers, his wife "Blondie," or a peddler at the front door, the titular head of the Bumstead household is almost always being galvanized into motion. Try to make skeleton figures of him in all these poses.

Mama and papa are dancing with joy in this cartoon of mine. Put them on a diet and see what their skeletons would look like.

"We heard!"

Everybody's in step here (I hope). Are *your* figures the same?

"And you, Harcomb—when were you bitten by the adventure bug?"

STRIPS FOR ACTION!

"Ferd'nand" gets the bird here as Danish cartoonist Henning Dahl Mikkelsen (Mik) puts him through the paces.

Fer'nand   **by Henning Dahl Mikkelsen**

© 1965 United Feature Syndicate, Inc.

"Superman," drawn by Wayne Boring, never was known for inactivity.

Superman   **by Wayne Boring**

© 1965 Bell-McClure Syndicate, Inc.

"Mutt and Jeff" have been kicking up the traces for over sixty years and here's Jeff livelier than ever in Al Smith's strip.

Mutt and Jeff   **Created by Bud Fisher**

© 1972 Aedita S. de Beaumont

Speaking of dancing, Fred Flintstone's no wallflower either. Try your skeleton figures on him and Miss Pebble while they dance the latest cave man cha-cha to music provided by a de luxe Stone Age hi-fi.

Look at Fred move here!

THE FLINTSTONES

By HANNA-BARBERA

Running, walking, standing, or kneeling, there is always "action" in Bud Blake's little figures in his kid strip, "Tiger."

Children being absolutely unpredictable, there's no telling anything about them—even what size to make 'em.

This feller is
3 heads tall

This gal is
4 heads tall

This guy is only
2 heads tall

In cartooning, ANYTHING can happen!

When we speak of a figure as having "good action", it doesn't necessarily mean jumping or running.

"Like to know what went wrong?"

I've tried to give the figures of these two yeggs "good action" although they are standing still.

© Esquire

The kid with the gun on him probably wished I had given him lots more action, like putting him on a train or somethin'!

© Esquire

"I believe you two have met"

Our next step is THE FATTENING UP PROCESS

Take your original skeleton figure

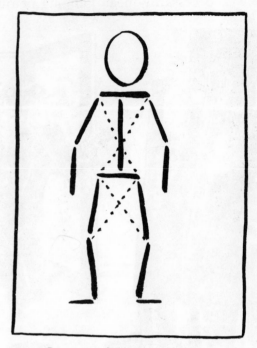

Draw supplementary lines as indicated

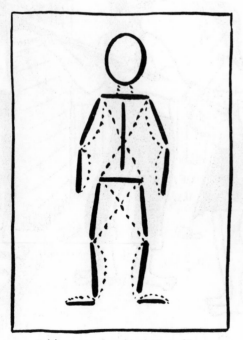

Add more supplementary lines

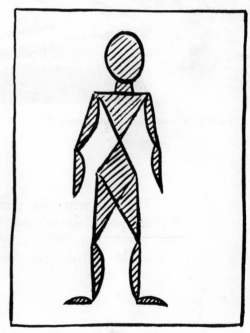

Tone in to get feeling of mass

Practice this exercise.

Do the same thing with *all* your skeletons.

Use a transparent tissue overlay to stroke in the action lines of the figures you have just done, with as few lines as possible. Simply place your tissue over the drawings on the preceding page, and select the lines *essential* to the action.

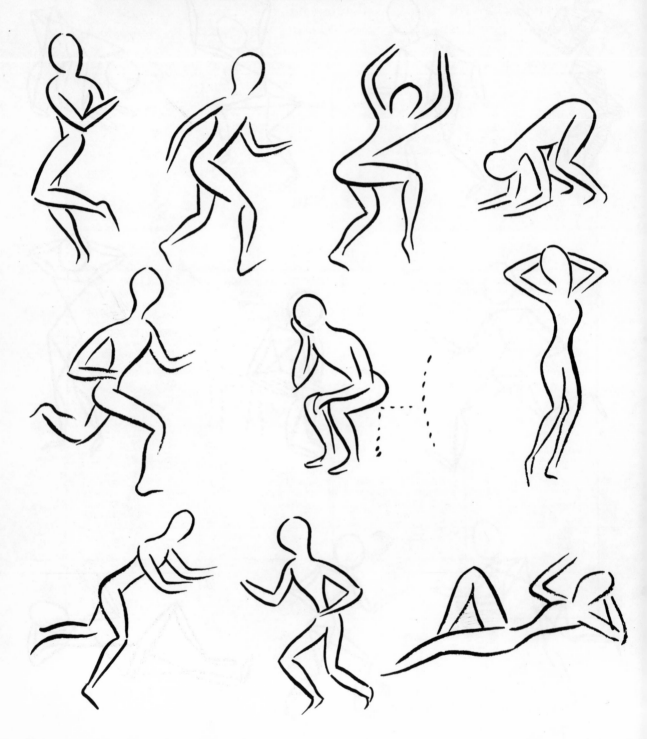

Got all that? Are you drawing like Michelangelo now? Are your figures in perfect proportion and recognizable to one and all? Oh, dear, perhaps you went to a lot of trouble for naught! Look at these three sample strips of Mell Lazarus' popular "Miss Peach." The children are all perfectly adorable but one can't tell where their spinal cords begin or end, or find their buttocks.

© 1972 Field Enterprises, Inc.

The reason for the success of this strip is, perhaps, that cartooning, like all great art forms, is flexible, and though there are established rules, from time to time we must expect someone to come along and break them—cutely, of course.

Here's a Buck Brown cartoon that's a real belly laugh.

"Gladys — is it really you?!"

"Can I call back? I'm right in the middle of someone."

"Doctor" Kaufman reminds us of a very important point— namely, that cartoonists and surgeons have one thing in common: Neither cares for complications! The surgeon doesn't want to run into gallstones when he's performing a tonsilectomy and the cartoonist being a man with a "message" mustn't let himself be sidetracked either. So—

KEEP IT SIMPLE!

One of the secrets of good cartooning is simplicity. People look at funny pictures for a chuckle, and should not be confused by a lot of unnecessary detail.

Take a hand, for example:  (An X-Ray picture no radiologist could take.)

This interesting appendage is composed of innumerable bones, phalanges, metacarpals, etc., etc., all of which are very vital and we're grateful for each and every. But for cartooning, all you have to know is that the average hand has five fingers except on leap years when there can be three or six.

Hands can be drawn this way and the medical profession can call in a doctor if they don't like:

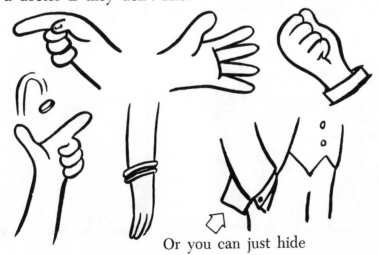

Or you can just hide 'em in a pocket.

This page should come in *handy*, eh? Ouch!

Feet may be complicated to chiropodists,* but not to cartoonists!

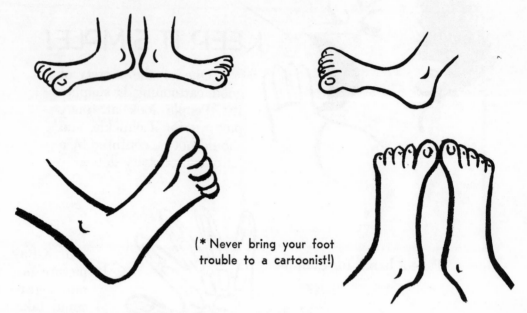

(* Never bring your foot
trouble to a cartoonist!)

You may get a kick out of drawing these.

SIMPLIFY EVERYTHING

This girl is almost lost
in the big city.

She now has a reasonable
chance of not winding up in
the Missing Persons Bureau.

WRONG

RIGHT

Too much attention is
attracted to the pipe.

This is better.

Practice simplifying objects as you draw them. Train yourself to look away from a thing and remember only its most important characteristics. It may be a bad habit to be forgetful, generally speaking—but not in cartooning!

The structure of a leaf is very interesting to botanists and followers of the trail. But for a cartoon—

—c'est tout!

4. COMPOSITION

H armony is a beautiful thing . . . in a song, among nations, and in a picture. Consciously or otherwise, we all try to make things pleasing to the eye. When you move into an apartment you don't just push your furniture in and have a housewarming. Everything is planned. Even the hanging of Grandpa's portrait is accomplished with deep thought and loving care (unless you just want him to cover a crack in the wall) and the humble ashtray doesn't reach its final resting place until after much deliberation and perhaps a few arguments.

Planning a picture is called Composition. Artists strive to make everything within a frame harmonious and decorative. Cartoonists go a step further. Like the director of a play or movie, they have to give their picture as much dramatic punch or sock as possible. And yet, at the same time, their artistic sensitivity will not permit them to abandon the basic laws of composition—good harmony and design.

RIGHT   WRONG

1.   2.

The composition in this picture is all right. But see what happens in the next picture—

By raising his hand, the young man has knocked the picture lopsided. (Can this be why teacher used to get mad when I raised my hand?)

The only way to restore good composition to picture No. 2 would be to balance it on the right by adding some object.

"Seventeen major European cities in twenty-one days."

Mischa Richter has arranged this picture so that our eye sweeps from left to right, pausing only at the uniformed officials, then on up the steps to the rest of the disembarking passengers—a masterful composition!

Mrs. Brown feels very blue here. It isn't the housework that's got her down—she just knows her composition is all wrong.

See how much better Mrs. Brown feels now. (It's the little things that make women happy!)

Things went well at the office for Mr. Brown, but he has a bad feeling on the right side (not his appendix) as he goes up the steps.

Ah, yes, there's nothing wrong with Mr. Brown now as Rover bounds into the picture and saves the composition.

The Browns are glaring at each other—something has happened to destroy the harmony of their home.

No wonder—the table was in the wrong place.

Maybe Johnny thinks he's better off alone in this picture—

—but we don't! (C'mon, Mom, let him have a cookie!)

Lefty enjoyed that soda, we bet, but we should've let him take a couple more steps before snapping him.

Nice of you to pose again, Lefty. And thanks for fixing the sidewalk.

Oh—oh! Lefty's catching it for eating before supper. Please, Pop, don't take him to the woodshed—

—just move him over near the window to improve the composition.

Here is an interesting exercise. In each of the cards on the right, we try to balance the two spots above with a different number of spots. Try this exercise, starting with any amount of spots placed anywhere.

The secretary in this drawing should only know her shorthand the way cartoonist Phil Interlandi knows his composition!

© True

"I know I haven't said anything. Read it back to me anyway."

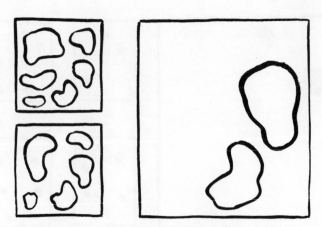

The same exercise, using large forms. Each time a new form is added the imagination is challenged to create a new design within the frame. Have fun.

"We-e-ll, madam—they're ALL good swimmers"   © D.A.C. News

One more canary cage in the window might have ruined this composition for me.

Junior saved his mother in this cartoon, but if that guy on the left hadn't shown up, I might have lost the balance of the whole picture!

© Esquire

"Don't do that again, Mother . . . I promise to write you more often"

What is the best way to start a cartoon? In my opinion before starting to plan a composition, a cartoonist must develop a mood regarding the drawing he is about to make. This mood will not only establish the feeling for the picture but be most important in helping him determine what to put into it.

For example, let us say the assignment is a nervous bookkeeper about to hit his boss up for a raise. I begin by thinking about both characters. After a while I have a good mental image of both and I begin sketching them.

Being an old friend of underdogs everywhere, the more I think of the bookkeeper, the sorrier I feel for him. I decide that it's taken the poor guy ten years to work up nerve enough to ask for this raise and that it's probably his wife's idea anyway.

Then I start thinking about the boss and perhaps I hear great roaring sounds of battle first. After the smoke clears away I see *him*, the Old Man—Harvard or Princeton '03, a vegetarian except for the fact that once in a while he eats nervous bookkeepers asking for a raise.

I decide to make it even tougher for the bookkeeper by making the boss real busy this day . . . lots of orders on his desk, five phones ringing, secretaries barging in and out . . . (aren't cartoonists sadistic?)

Will the bookkeeper get the raise? Will the boss say yes or throw him out of the 84th-floor window? For the answer to this and other startling questions turn to the next page.

Having established the two characters in my mind, I now proceed to make rough sketches of the situation.

My problem now is to figure out which composition is best and then to do a finish.

(P.S. He got the raise!)

The average cartoonist would panic if called upon to make a drawing showing two ladies gazing askance at one of those new glass skyscrapers, but Robert Day is noted for the ease with which he handles the most difficult composition.

"They'll never get <u>me</u> under one of those things!"

"I've never seen him in this bad a mood."

If the umpire had thumbed everybody out of the picture on the left before the others, I would have been in real trouble here.

A comic strip cartoonist must solve the problems of composition in each and every box as Dale Messik shows here in her famous strip "Brenda Starr," perfectly integrating main characters, "balloons," and backgrounds.

Brenda Starr   by Dale Messik

© 1972 The Chicago Tribune

Take a tip from Dale Messik. Keep incidental figures and backgrounds subdued so as not to detract from your main characters. Try to develop the art of simplifying by studying an object, then drawing only its most important characteristics—IN AS FEW LINES AS POSSIBLE.

And if you're beginning to think these lessons are for the birds, perhaps cartoonist Ed Nofziger agrees.

for the birds by ED NOFZIGER

"When I gaze deep into your eyes something happens to me. I get sleepy."

"No, not married. Just clumsy!"

"Just about the time we manage to get a nest egg, more bills accumulate!"

© Parade

5. PERSPECTIVE

The vanishing point is not a place where cartoonists wish their editors would go. It is an expression used in connection with that myopic phenomenon called "perspective."

Perspective plays a large part in almost any drawing and even cartoonists follow its laws.

This is the most ancient example of perspective and I blush to repeat it:

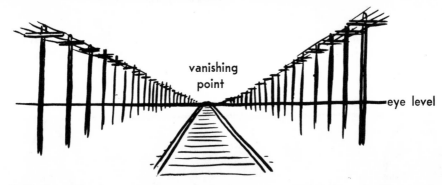

"All the telephone poles are the same size and the tracks evenly apart. But to the eye they are not. The poles and the tracks get smaller and smaller the farther away they are. This is called the vanishing point."

These might be the exact words of Leonardo da Vinci in the 15th century if only the railroad had gone past his house.

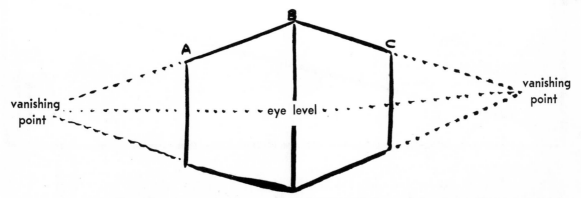

A still earlier ancestor once noted that all the sides of this house are the same height but B is larger than A or C because it is nearest our line of vision.

Other savants have taken note that a boy like this ain't *really* bigger than his papa—he only *appears* to be! What won't they think up next?

The bartender didn't actually give A a bigger beer for his money than B. It just looks that way or B would let out a holler. (A guy named C, standing farther up the bar, got even a smaller looking beer but he thought he saw his wife coming and left for the vanishing point.)

This drawing by Al Kaufman perfectly illustrates one man's hysteria and a whole street's perspective.

© True

"Fred, Fred, have a heart! You'll louse up the whole vacation schedule!"

Ned Hilton's counter would disappear into a vanishing point, if it didn't swing around toward that other guy in back.

"*If you're going to look so peevish every morning, I might as well eat breakfast at home.*"   © Look

Henry Boltinoff's patient doesn't know if the consultant they called in is really a "big man" or just looks small because he's farther away.

"Just makeup. This is being televised."   © Elks Magazine

A perfect example of perspective by master cartoonist Mischa Richter.

"It's a terminal case—he's broke."

Observe the laws of perspective even if Congress repeals them!

6. TECHNIQUE

All right, then! Having devoured the book's contents up to this point, and practiced the prescribed exercises very diligently, I hereby pronounce sentence upon you: YOU ARE NOW A CARTOONIST! So welcome to the fold! And may all your troubles be funny ones.

You are ready to make finished cartoons. But before you can declare yourself "Open For Business," a small but necessary investment must be made. Up to this point in your life you have patronized drug stores, candy stores, clothing stores, hat stores, and shoe stores. There is a new one to add to your list—The Art Supply Store. Break open your piggy bank and go to the nearest one.

Don't be shy about going into an art supply store. According to vital statistics, most hands squeezing tubes of paint these days are amateur ones. And the average dealer I know is a strange merchant in one respect—he is really and sincerely interested in helping his customers. Explain the nature of the work you have planned and then, depending on your budget, let him help you make the following selection:

A suitable drawing board	A ruler
An assortment of camel hair brushes	Scissors
India Ink (comes in all colors as well as black)	Mixing tray
A tube of lampblack water color	Tracing pads
Chinese White	Pencil Sharpener
Erasers—sand ones and kneaded	Etc.
Pencils—hard and soft	

Modern art supply stores contain the most wonderful materials for making your work as comfortable and pleasant as possible. A far cry, indeed, from the days when old masters had to make their own pigments!

At any rate, the things you purchase are the tools of your craft. Take care of them, and, with luck, they'll take care of you. Set your drawing board up in a place where there is a good light. A lot of interesting things can be done in the dark. Drawing is not one of them.

There are two main techniques for finished cartoons: line and wash. The line drawing can be just as it sounds, or be done with ben-day (an engraving process), crayon, or just pen and ink. Wash tones are achieved by mixing two ingredients—black water color and H_2O. The less water, the deeper the tone, and vice versa.

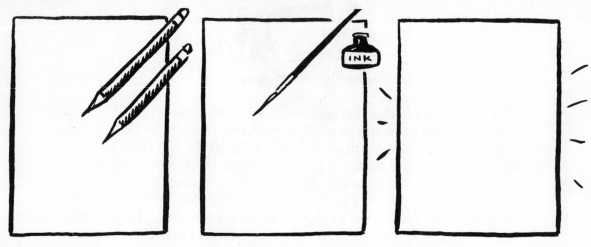

Preliminary Sketch. Use soft pencil at first, then slightly harder one when you see line you want.

Ink in. When finished use kneaded eraser to eliminate pencil lines and sand eraser for possible ink mistakes.

What you have now is a Line Drawing!

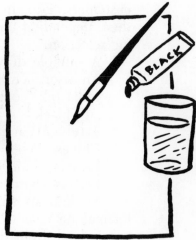

Some line drawings are augmented with pen and ink, black crayon or spatter-brush (tooth brush dipped in ink).

Ben Day. Indicate with blue pencil or light blue wash where you want engraver to make gray tone.

Wash drawing. A greater variety and softness of tones is obtained with this medium but it is not feasible with some artists' styles.

Expert handling of line by Mischa Richter lets us feel third-dimensional quality in this drawing without the use of tones or shading.

Bob Day uses many techniques. This one is wash.

Good, sound drawing accompanies the lucid style of line cartoonist Al Ross.

"I'm amazed at how relaxed you can be, knowing the future and all that."

"Admit it. You're scared to death of me!"

These are the delightfully zany line drawings of Virgil Partch ("Vip").

© True

"You don't love our children."

© Colliers

"Homesick?"

"I left my topcoat here last night."

© Look

"Are you sure you can afford
toys for another child?"

"One of us has a screw loose!"

"Then when Clara Bow didn't
answer your father's letters,
he turned to me."

"I thought you were supposed
to go down with the ship."

These are line draw-
ings for my one-column,
daily newspaper feature,
"Laugh It Off."

"Would you mind settling an
argument? Was it last week
or the week before that you
got a hit?"

"Do you mind telling me how
that delicious chef's salad I
had in the dining car was
prepared?"

This   cartoon   for   a
magazine is also in line,
augmented   with   crayon
shading.

"Well, what's it gonna be tonight? Brain surgery on N.B.C. or
an appendectomy on C.B.S.?"

Mr. and Mrs. George Smith used "line" entirely for this edition of "The Smith Family."

The Smith Family by Mr. and Mrs. George Smith

Rupe is another cartoonist who uses "line" for his strip.

FREDDY by RUPE

Zack Mosley simply used "line" for this strip, too.

Smilin' Jack by Zack Mosley

TRUDY

3-14   © King Features Syndicate, Inc., 1972. World rights reserved.

Jerry Marcus

"So you used your after-shave lotion before and your before lotion after. SO WHAT?"

Jerry Marcus used ben-day in these panels from his popular newspaper feature.

TRUDY

"I'll tell ya what I learned in school today—I learned my teacher can read lips!"

TRUDY

"Trudy? Marge Gentry called—she wanted to know if you heard about that sale downtown!"

I did this drawing in wash too, again using crayon for added "texture."

"He said to tell you he was hanged this morning"

Two more wash draw-
ings of mine.

"... *but not so built-up that I become muscle-bound*"

Wash is an acceptable
medium at most magazines.

"*I always have too much month left over at the end of the money*"

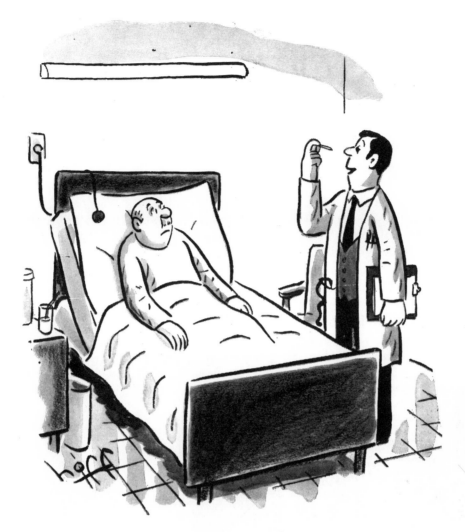

"Well, well, just like Amalgamated Copper—one hundred and one and a half."

Finding a technique best suited to yourself may take some time. Try them all—and enjoy experimenting until you find one particular method that seems easiest and gives you the best results.

But even then, don't ever feel wedded exclusively to any particular way of doing a drawing. All the great cartoonists you have seen in this book so far are constantly pulling surprises, both on their legions of readers and themselves. One never knows just exactly what technique they will use in their next drawings—line, wash, crayon, or ben-day. They experiment constantly, and this is what keeps their work fresh-looking, vigorous, and in demand.

7. HOW TO GET CARTOON IDEAS

The gold nuggets of this industry are, of course, the ideas—or gags—and if you think Sutter was elated when he struck pay dirt in '49, you should see a cartoonist when he finally dreams up one that he thinks will sell.

"Where do you get your ideas?" is the question most often thrown at every brush and pen pusher in the trade. And never does the poor guy look readier for the nuthouse than when he's trying to think of the answer. Where do *I* get my ideas? Why, they come from, er . . . you see, that is, . . . er . . . hey, fellers, move over!

"If I knew where I got my ideas, I'd be there right now getting them," the immortal Milt Gross, creator of Nize Baby, That's My Pop, Count Screwloose, and Dave's Delicatessen once said wistfully to a group of us kids in a high school art class long ago.

"Did you put out that cigarette back at camp?"

I was nowhere near Smokey the Bear when I got this idea. I just happened to be looking at my uncle who's got an awful lot of hair on his chest.

Let's face it. Ideas are often hard to get. The fellow who tells you they aren't is probably either just being modest or he's stealing them from somebody else.

"I've got a great idea for you," friends will say when they learn you're a cartoonist, and you'll listen patiently, trying to keep that pained look off your face. "Not bad—not bad at all," you'll murmur. But your friends will be hurt by your lack of enthusiasm and they'll *never* give you another idea for a cartoon—not until next time.

The longer you stay in the business the grimmer the task of getting good ideas becomes. At parties people will be amazed to learn that the morose individual sitting alone in the corner—perhaps with a gun pressed against his temple—is the celebrated cartoonist who turns out all those very funny jokes.

All right, so cartoonists are not necessarily clowns. How do they get their ideas? More important, how can you, a beginner, get them?

If someone suddenly invited you to invest in a Montana sheep ranch, you'd insist on learning something about it first, wouldn't you? You'd probably feel the same way if you were going into plumbing, textiles, or any one of a hundred other businesses.

The gag business is no different. A reasonable amount of background is necessary if you are going to try this strange, new occupation. How can you go about acquiring it? Here are some suggestions:

1. Start looking closely at the cartoons appearing in current periodicals.
2. Read and study cartoon anthologies to learn what's been published in the past. These can be found in bookstores or public libraries.
3. Get to know all these cartoons reasonably well.
4. Make a note of certain situations you observe recurring, and save them for future reference.

You might have observed that in wading through such a vast mountain of cartoons that you laughed hardest at those situations most familiar to you, or those with which you could *identify*. For instance, if you are connected with a fire department, a joke about a lady being carried down a ladder while she's still gabbing on the phone probably amused you. If you are connected with an airline, you could have liked the one showing a male passenger flirting with the gal next to him and explaining that he has to work fast because the jet's going so fast, they'll be landing almost before they meet.

This "identifying" is a good symptom. It shows you have an affinity for a certain type of joke. Give your mind free rein and try to think of amusing incidents along that particular line. In humor, as in all fields of creative endeavor, there is no substitute for experience.

After a certain amount of time has been spent studying cartoons intently, you should be starting to "think funny." (This is a normal reaction. If you spend enough time in a Chinese laundry, you'll get used to starched shirts.)

SOME WAYS NOT TO GET GAGS FOR CARTOONS

Stand on your head.

Become an AAA
statistic.

Pull all your hair out.

Go crazy.

Consult your notes and select one of those recurring situations you noticed always turning up in cartoons. Let's say it is the most commonly used situation of all—the one about the shipwrecked boy and girl.

Study some of the hundreds of lines already done for this situation.

"What I mean is you're the nicest girl I've met *recently*."

"How long do you want to keep our engagement a secret?"

"I know you told me your name last week. Can't you tell me again?"

"I wish you'd look at me when you talk."

"Do you mind if I try again, this time using a different approach?"

"Don't worry, the Internal Revenue people will find us. They'd never let me get away with my taxes this easily."

"Do you mean we'll just have to go on sitting here like this until I find a minister?"

"If my wife should come along, please don't mention a word about this to her."

"I wish you had brought along a canasta deck."

"Take a letter to the Blue Star Shipping Company, Miss Jones."

"Your husband sounds like a very interesting person. Tell me more about him."

"I can't help thinking of that book I took out of the library back home. The fine is going to be enormous."

"Eight months now and I still can't think of what I'll tell my wife."

"How would you like your eggs this morning?"

Now you try to think up a line of your own to fit that cartoon. Try the line on your wife—or a friend. See their reaction. If they don't laugh, keep thinking and try another line on them. You may be making a pest of yourself but—too bad—there's no way to avoid this.

Move on to the next "old situation." Let's say that this time it's the one about the hubby coming home late, being met in the doorway by his angry wife.

Do the same as before. Study some of the lines already used in this situation.

"Did anybody ever tell you you're beautiful when you're angry?"

"If you must know, I was celebrating our anniversary."

"You're always asking where I'd be if I hadn't married you. That's where I was."

"Of all the houses in the neighborhood, I had to pick Elizabeth Taylor's!"

"Before you go flying off the handle, dear, would you mind checking my Blue Cross?"

"I know I got the wrong house, lady. I just wanted to try out my alibi on you before I go home."

"Darling, I thought you'd be deep in your beauty sleep."

"Now, take it easy, dear, remember what the neighbors said last time you lost your temper."

"I'm trying to remember. Did we kiss and make up when I left the house this morning, or are we still mad?"

"Well, I'm the husband of *somebody* on this block!"

Once again try to make your wife (if she's still married to you), or a friend laugh with a line of your own origin. And if you have success—horrors! What have I done? It was tough enough selling cartoons without having more competition!

You might think Ned Hilton had to go abroad to get this gag, but the truth is that he got it while nursing a beer on Eighth Avenue in New York's Manhattan.

"I wish we were back home with the neighbors who wish they could be here."

© Look

Reamer Keller got this idea one day when his battery needed charging.

© Farm Journal

"No, I think I'd rather have the engine up front between me and whatever I hit."

Cartoonist Frank Modell thought up this idea while worrying about the national crime situation.

"There must be some mistake. We've already been robbed."

I don't know *how* I got this idea, but it must have been Saturday night.

"I object, your Honor! Counsel is leading the witness!"

The best system for getting ideas is to work at it. Sometimes they will come so easy and fast there is no stopping them. During these delightful periods there'll be extra large tips for the waitress and barber, a kind word and pat on the head for all the neighborhood children. And you'll be able to shave without wanting to cut your throat. But in those other stretches?

People will pull their young away when they see you approaching, and dogs will hide. Your wife will wonder what's come over you. Her mother will tell her she should have married that other guy. You'll rue the day you ever went in for cartooning and wonder whether it's too late for you to get back into that other business where people seemed so nice and normal. However, just when you're ready to quit, the gags will start coming again. Sound maddening? Heck, yes—but there isn't a man in the business who'd give it up! (Make me an offer!)

My wife was trying on a zebra-striped bikini when I got this idea.

"Oh, there you are!"

I thought of this when a neighbor of ours announced she was going on a diet.

"To put it into language you can understand Mrs. Green, you eat too damned much!"

*"When the pioneers came through here a hundred years ago, you can bet
they didn't care whether or not a motel had color television."*

© 1962 The New Yorker Magazine, Inc.

The professional gag hunter doesn't wait for inspiration to strike.
He is out looking for ideas all the time, frequently finding stimulus
in looking at other people's drawings. In addition to learning what
the markets are buying this way, his busy mind explores each picture
with a scrutiny that would do justice to an agent from Scotland Yard.

No stone is left unturned as he looks for a clue that will lead him to
a gag of his own. For example, looking at the above drawing he
might start thinking of something completely different, perhaps something already going on in Cabin 3 there in the background—a man
arguing with his wife. No, it isn't his wife—it's his secretary. She
forgot to bring along her notebook. No, perhaps it's the secretary
who's sore—she's already seen the picture they're showing on television. Television? A repair man is coming in to fix the set. Set? The

gag man thinks of a woman setting her hair. No, she just came from the beauty shop and unless she shows him a receipt, her husband won't believe it. Believe? The police never believe a suspect. Suspect? A couple are in front of a jewelry store window, the fellow's arm raised with a brick in it: "See anything you like, honey?" Honey? Bees in a honeycomb, one saying to the other: "You must give me a buzz sometime." Sometime? The boss is sore because Jones keeps watching the clock. . . .

Where will this all end? When you start "snowballing," there's no telling!

Within each of us, if we are creative, there is a natural reservoir of ideas waiting to be tapped. The trick is to have a faucet that can be turned on at will.

But suppose the well runs dry or the plumbing breaks down? Or suppose you only have a flair for cartooning, or drawing, and are not actually "creative" as far as ideas are concerned? Don't despair. There are scores of professional writers who, for a percentage of your check, will come to your rescue. And there are enough of these people to send you correspondence to make your mailman wish you had never been born. Let's find out about a few of these "gag writers," and what they—and their products—are like:

Habitat plays a big part in determining what kind of cartoons you will do. I grew up in the asphalt jungle of the city, so in most of my drawings you might get the feeling there's a danger of falling plaster. If you grew up in the wide-open spaces, your work will undoubtedly have an altogether different flavor from mine.

"I don't feel like watching the fights. I'd rather watch a Western."

"In two months you'll be able to talk back to anybody—no matter who she is."

High atop California's Pacific Palisades, Ben Cassell sits, grinding out gags and watching his wife ride a surfboard in the ocean below. Ben's been at it 22 years, believes his best stuff to be the ones he's never sold, but he's connected over 5,000 times and here are some of those he considers his best:

Man to information clerk in railroad station: "Why am I here? What does all this mean in the infinite scheme of things?" (*The Post*) . . . Woman with a new baby in hospital bed talks to friend: "It wasn't a bit like the book." (*Ladies Home Journal*) . . Man to angry Senator at press conference outside Senate building: "Senator, will you blow your top over foreign aid once more for the benefit of the staff photographers?" (*The New Yorker*).

Cliff Fitton of Bridgeport, Connecticut, has found 95 per cent of the cartoonists he deals with honest. (His remarks about the other 5 per cent cannot appear in this book.) Here are some of Cliff's best gags:

College president angrily to big guy with football sweater: "We feel that your expulsion will teach you a valuable lesson about making costly fumbles in life." (*Sports Illustrated*) . . . As husband on street lifts hat to shapely babe passing by, wife lifts up his wig. No caption. (*The Post*) . . . Woman driver to motorcycle cop writing out traffic summons: "You wouldn't dare talk to me like that if you didn't have a gun." (*American Legion*) . . . Disheveled stenog coming out of boss's office, saying to young gal going in: "Be careful of him today.

He's in a good mood." (*The New Yorker*) . . . Brother Sebastian, the religious monk, throwing worms from a can to fish in pond with sign "No Fishing." (*Look*)

Another standout gag man is Brooklyn's Irving Cohen, who authored such *New Yorker* dillies as:

The gal saying to a marriage license clerk: "Anybody get stood up today?" . . . Hubby to wife drilling hole in wall: "Couldn't you just eavesdrop dear?" And the captionless pushcart peddler selling "Fresh Fish" dressed as a deep sea diver.

Other gems by this unsung genius are:

The pair of parrots at a wild party saying, "Let's go somewhere where we can talk." (*This Week*) . . . Bank official to employee: "Can't I turn my head for a moment without someone embezzling a million dollars?" (*Liberty*) . . . Kid painting a green apple red before giving it to his teacher. (*The Post*) . . . Kid buying a penny lollypop, telling the storekeeper: "Wrap it as a gift." (*King Features*)

"You must be making plans
for your husband's vacation."

"He's not much to look at but he's
worth his weight in pennies."

This idea came to cartoonist Barney Tobey one day at noon, when his fancy was lightly turning to thoughts of lunch.

"I can't understand you, Harold. Why is it you're the only one who doesn't know it's spring?"

Herb Gochros of Westport, Connecticut, sells about six hundred gags a year—like:

A worried-looking female rabbit saying to her husband, "Of course we could adopt some." (*The New Yorker*) . . . A bride saying to another guy as she leaves church with the groom: "Didn't you get my note?" (*Look*) . . . Big sign "Beware of Dog" next to tiny Pekinese as mistress explains to friend: "We put it up to bolster Fifi's morale." (*The Post*)

In Creve Coeur, Missouri, Arnot Sheppard has been grinding them out for a quarter of a century:

Woman telling her analyst: "It's certainly a relief to talk to you, doctor—you're the only person I don't feel inferior to." (*Playboy*) . . . Kid with books: "I guess I can't complain. I had a rich full life before I started school." (*Cartoons of the Month*) . . . Knights in armor fleeing the dragon shooting fire at them one knight saying: "Feels good though, doesn't it?" (*The New Yorker*) . . . Woman complaining to her book-reading husband: "You know what I think? I think you're purposely being intellectual." (*The New Yorker*) . . . Indian squaw serving husband who's busy watching television: "Your grandfather hunted the buffalo to fill his stomach, but you can't even get your own TV dinner!" (*Cartoons of the Month*) . . . Wife of minister yelling at him: "Don't turn your other cheek to me." (*The New Yorker*) . . . Woman jurors: "It may have been irrelevant, incompetent, and immaterial but it was certainly juicy." (*The New Yorker*)

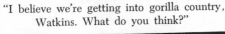

"I believe we're getting into gorilla country,
Watkins. What do you think?"

Still another operator in this off-beat profession is Art Paul whose "Laughs Unlimited" has sold everything in the humor line from a parody of "Old Man River" called "One Man's Liver," to the speeches of a dozen congressmen and leading industrialists. Cartoon-wise, Art has been responsible for such ideas as:

A sultan's baby son playing with little girls, asking his father, "How'm I doing, Pop?" . . . A two-headed girl backstage phoning, "Hello, Mom— I got the part!" . . . Old duffer boasting to another as butler wheels in large cake, "It's an old recipe that was handed down by my grandmother." . . . A lady telling her marriage counselor, "Oh, we get along all right, but not with each other." . . . Card players in nudist colony, one saying, "Wanna have some fun? Let's get dressed and play strip poker." . . . Attractive girl visiting her boyfriend behind bars, complains to him, "Other convicts talk to their girlfriends. They don't just sit there and think."

H. BOLTINOFF

"It clashes with my salary!"

© Parade

All these gag men and the dozens of others in this business get their ideas by hard work. You can do the same, if you apply yourself. Here are some further suggestions that might be helpful:

"My mother doesn't understand me."

"These guys must be real Indians—
that rain dance is working!"

1. Keep up with the news. Topical or timely events can frequently be converted into gags.

2. Imagine *yourself* as the star in every conceivable situation. How would *you* react if you were a sultan and had 58 wives? Suppose you were on a safari and the elephants charged?—got shipwrecked with a beautiful blonde?—found yourself on a honeymoon with a tattooed lady?—had a wife who gave birth to quintuplets?—stumbled into a nudist camp by mistake?—loaned your neighbor a lawn mower and he didn't return it?—discovered that the patient you're about to operate on is your old army sergeant?—heard your clock going tock-tick instead of tick-tock?—blew a mating call in the woods and your wife answered?—were a schoolteacher and the rich kid brought you a mink coat instead of an apple?—had to listen to the heartbeat of a French poodle? . . .

Put yourself in the middle of all these settings, and a million others, and try to figure it out from there. Cartooning is a happy work. Wanna bet you'll have fun?

8. HOW TO SELL YOUR CARTOONS

We will suppose that you have reached the point where you are ready to make a first presentation of your work. How should you go about doing this? Should you check your underarm deodorant? Take a course in public speaking? Run out and buy a new suit? I say, by all means do those things. But for Pete's sake, they aren't necessary as far as selling your cartoons is concerned. Editors are very busy people and it's asking too much to suppose that they will stop the presses every time a new cartoonist wanders in with down on his cheek and a portfolio in his hand. Besides, it is unlikely that you or your personality will have anything to do with the sale of your work. Anybody can sell a cartoon—*as long as it's good!*

How then should you make that presentation? The answer is very simple. If you live in the city where a particular publication is located, or within reasonable proximity, find out what day the editor sees contributors. Then drop in and—get on line. However, if you live far away from the publication, mail in your work. Just remember to be sure and enclose a stamped, self-addressed envelope.

"Will work mailed in really get looked at?" you might ask. Most assuredly, yes. You may rest assured that editors peruse very carefully every contribution they receive. It is to their advantage, as well as yours, to make "new discoveries." An editor who comes up with a bright new star in the firmament of comic art becomes known as "on the ball." He is waiting to discover you—if you are worth discovering.

Let me elaborate. Public fancies change all the time, and editors know this better than anybody else. They know that old cartoonists have a habit of becoming "old hat." They go out of style. Their characters become dated. The editor cannot go on accepting them because they belong to another era. He must tap the new lode of talent, corner the new genius before a rival editor beats him to it.

Does the word "editor" strike fear in your heart? Calm yourself. I have known a hundred cartoon editors in my time and can vouch that not one of them resembled Count Dracula—well, *almost* none of them. As a matter of fact, most editors are extremely kind and sympathetic, and deplore their position of sitting in judgment like Lord High Executioners. What, then, are they really like?

Premier market in the entire cartoon empire and the one most cartoonists aspire to attain is *The New Yorker*. Here where the pay is highest and prestige greatest, most of the original All-Stars still dominate the pages—Steig, Arno, Addams, etc. However, enough new names make their debut in this sophisticated magazine annually to warrant classifying it as "wide open."

White-thatched Jim Geraghty, the editor—a former gag man himself—when asked what he looks for in a cartoon, stares moodily at the view of Manhattan's canyons from his office window and says: "Other editors may be able to articulate what it is they want. I cannot, except to say that I want desperately something I have never seen and never dreamed of. I am constantly hoping to be surprised."

Perhaps some will feel that editor Geraghty owes a fuller explanation, perhaps even a blueprint of what it is he seeks. (Would that he could supply one!) None, however, can deny the great contribution his magazine has made to modern cartooning, both in drawing styles and humor. A perusal of *New Yorker* anthologies easily reveals this and all practitioners of the art should know that they are forever in its debt.

The late Gurney Williams, of *Look*, was considered the Dean of cartoon editors. He labored "way back when," in the vineyards of *College Humor, Judge,* the old *Life,* and *Colliers.*

© Look

"How can I enjoy this vacation? I keep thinking of my boss
messing up the files looking for something."

Williams might even have been with Bret Harte in those old frontier days when 'tis said cartoonists drew on each other for gag stealing (as well as hoss thievery). Williams offered these sobering remarks on a subject dear to his heart: "Thirty years ago there were a lot of magazines devoted primarily to cartoons, the artistic quality of which was often doubtful. Today's market calls for better drawing, brighter ideas. In this extremely competitive field only the skillful artist with the individual style reaches the top. Engineers, doctors, and astronauts succeed only after intensive study and preparation. Successful cartoonists will tell you that they too spent years perfecting their techniques.

"YOU SHOULDN'T BE DOING THAT, DAD. LET ME TAKE IT DOWN TO THE CAR WASH PLACE FOR YOU!"

© American Youth

"You may have a flair that can be developed until you become a cartoon great. If so, study, work, observe what goes on around you. Draw, draw, draw. Then draw some more. And some day—surely not next week or next month—your name will be a Name."

Jerry Beatty is cartoon editor at *Esquire:* "I am a little put out when some newcomer shows up with drawings and casually says, 'I've decided to be a cartoonist in my spare time,' or mails them to me without a return envelope and often without an address, and asks for criticism. That kind of approach is unfair to the others.

"My advice to a beginner would be to learn not only something about the mechanics of art but also about the human factors. Most cartoonists are dedicated, hard-working guys who love what they're doing, and there must be something to love in it for wild horses can't drag them away from it.

"So, newcomer, take a shot at it. If you make it, it's fun. If you don't—well, let's not think about that."

"Good reasons why I shouldn't have a shipboard romance with you? One, you're my husband!"

Week after week the cartoon editor of the *Saturday Evening Post*, Michael Mooney, sifts reams of drawings sent in by eager contributors and occasionally the maddening hunt for good material pays off for him. Says Mooney: "The bus was headed downtown. I had a vantage point by the window behind two handsome women. The delicate one on the aisle had a copy of the *Post* open on her lap. She probably had a daughter who was a freshman in college, but she looked much younger. As she idled through the pages to choose what she would read, I shifted in my seat so that I might watch her better. She had stopped in the fiction section. She bent her head to read the caption of a cartoon. I knew which one absorbed her. Her head jerked up, she squinted and roared. It was a startling laugh—not the laugh of a suburban matron, but the laugh of a stevedore. It filled the bus. Passengers turned to see why she had exploded. Its echoes still ring for me.

"A cartoon editor is dedicated to that laugh and its cousins: the slow smile, the silly giggle, and the whoop of recognition. They are the joyous reward for the long hours of drudgery."

"Whoever's driving pull over to the curb."

"I told him I'd rather fight than rewrite."

Lawrence Lariar knows all the pitfalls. He is a cartoonist himself, bought cartoons for the late *Liberty* magazine, is now humor editor of *Parade*, the Sunday supplement. "In more than fifteen years of editing cartoons for national magazines, I have interviewed hundreds of amateur and professional cartoonists. On the basis of this experience I can afford to generalize about comic artists in general—and amateurs in particular. Here are a few rules of the game:

"1. Remember cartooning is an art form that cannot be mastered overnight. It must be studied with as much concentration and ardor as any other profession.

"2. *When submitting material to magazines or syndicates, do it the professional way!* Most beginners kill their chances early in the game by screaming their amateurism at the cartoon editor. The comic art business has established certain methods for submitting material. Make sure you follow the rules.

"3. *Never gripe before an editor!* Over the years I have witnessed many beginning cartoonists commit suicide by exposing themselves as hopeless paranoids. Never tell an editor that your work is as funny and as well drawn as most of the work he buys and prints!

"4. *Be patient with yourself!* If you have developed your talent to its maximum, never give up."

(Ed. note: Larry has made more than his share of cartoonist discoveries, as witness in his great series of anthologies, *Best Cartoons of the Year*.)

© D.A.C. Magazine

"Never mind the way you heard it"

"We've called in a consultant."

The Gag Re-Cap (Box 86, East Meadow, N.Y. 11554) is a trade publication that demonstrates the never-ending switching of cartoon ideas. One of its subscribers, J. I. Peyser, a part-time gag man, offers these: Tycoon to doctor, "I'm shocked that you gave me artificial respiration—I can afford the real thing." Sleepy man answering phone in middle of the night, "You've got the wrong idiot, you number!" Two men walking down street don't see an open manhole; one says, "In today's society, we could drop from sight and never be heard from again." Married couple arguing, woman says, "See, we can't even agree on the cause of this argument." Wife doing laundry holds up husband's shirt: "Congratulations, you've just invented a dirt that's stronger than bleach!"

John Bailey bought cartoons for the *Saturday Evening Post;* then *Suburbia Today* and *Family Weekly* employed his talents. Says he: "We will begin by assuming that you are a very funny fellow, and that you have a salable gag in mind. In fact, we will assume that you have already drawn your salable gag and that it has been rejected by ten markets. Why? There are a number of possible reasons but the most likely is that you haven't handled the gag properly.

"First, the drawing must be convincing. If there is any element in the cartoon which is impossible most readers will realize it subconsciously. And their subconscious reasoning will go as follows: 'Since this detail could not happen, then nothing is happening and there is nothing to laugh at.'

"A second important factor in a cartoon is simplicity. The rule is: Put in *everything* you need to show the humor fully. And put in *nothing* you don't need to show the humor fully.

"The most dangerous moment arrives when you get an okay. A common error is to decide to give the editor his money's worth. Everything that was funny in the rough goes, and in its place appears a solemn, careful drawing of tall, handsome people and a merchandised rendering of props.

"Remember that the editor liked your rough. Fix anything distracting but keep the characters and use the props to identify the scene, nothing more."

The Detroit Athletic Club is an exclusive organization with its own monthly periodical. Its editor was Robert B. Johnstone. "A good cartoon is like a happy marriage. Art is wedded to humor and if they both contribute talent, the couple lives happily ever after. We do not buy a well-drawn cartoon that is not funny nor do we buy a funny cartoon that is poorly drawn.

"But if there is a breadwinner to this marriage, it is the artist; it is the artist who gets his foot in the editor's door and, if his work is good, gets his product to the editor's desk for consideration. The funniest cartoons in the world will not even get this far if the drawing is so poor that a single glance at one sample rejects the whole package. If the wedding has not yet come off, perhaps these two aids will speed the happy day: First, develop a cartoon style of your own; all successful cartoonists are stylists rather than superb artists. Second, recognize early in the game if you are not funny and turn to a collaborator or professional gag writer; some cartoonists are funny, some are not, and a few of the latter never learn to admit it."

Charles Preston is the shrewd editor who buys cartoons for the *Wall Street Journal* and *National Observer*. "We *need* new cartoons . . . artists who combine draftsmanship and keen social commentary. A sound background is required; school, life-classes, and study the masters. Dürer, Hogarth, Rowlandson, Daumier. . . .

"Cartoonists should have something to say—something more than cliché gags. Though there will always be a market for gags, the cartoonist should essay a more important role. I think his function is also to comment on the world around him, and when necessary, puncture the pomposities that beset us.

"You must develop a style—your individual way of making your statement. This usually arrives with the ease of handling your materials, ideas and drawing, and when your style emerges and what you have to say is true—editors and readers will be grateful to you."

Newspapers have special restrictions, according to Bob Schroeter who buys 300 cartoons a year for King Features' "Laff-A-Day." "The cartoon must appeal to the reader without offending," he says. "Automatically eliminated are gags dealing with religion, liquor, mayhem, sex, insanity, suicide, and other subjects that seem to be increasing in magazine popularity. Gags also have to be selected with the thought in mind of the many advertisers. Known products can't be satirized. Many cartoonists wonder from time to time why a very funny gag knocking a used-car dealer didn't sell here. There are other reasons why a funny gag may be rejected, A topical gag covering a subject not *nationally* known is one that comes to mind.

"I guess what it all boils down to is that cartoons for newspapers should have family appeal and not be offensive."

There it is, right from the horses' mouths. All you need now are the names and addresses of some of the periodicals using cartoons, and you'll find such a list in the back of the book under Markets.

"As good as new? Couldn't you make him a little better?"   © D.A.C. Magazine

"And now for the part of this job I didn't tell you about . . . hands up!"

"Before I show you this report card, I'd like to ask you to remember how
cute I looked in my baby pictures."

While you're waiting to hear from these markets, dear young hopeful, don't waste time fretting. Get busy thinking up a new batch of gags. If you get the old ones back with a rejection slip, send them on to the next market. However, if the gods are smiling and an "okay" comes fluttering out of your package, bear these things in mind:

1. Be careful of low overhang if you are the type that jumps with joy.
2. Wait until your heart stops pounding before starting to draw.
3. Don't take narcotics to steady your hand.
4. Draw about twice the size of reproduction, unless instructed otherwise.
5. Use white illustration board—available in one, two, or more plies at any art supply store.
6. Remember what all those editors just told you.

And—Good luck!

"The doc says any time we get here before dark we gotta disguise our truck like an ambulance."

9. HOW TO SELL YOUR CARTOONS TO ADVERTISERS

From time to time the advertising spaces in the public press are brightened by the appearance of cartoons. Public reaction to this must be favorable because the use of humor in ad campaigns, a form of "soft sell," seems to be on the increase. Perhaps this is so because the H-bomb age is the age of distrust and apathy. People either don't believe what they're told, or they don't care. In any case, cartoonists are happy to find themselves in demand. The agencies pay handsomely for their services and far from resenting this crass commercialization of their talents, cartoonists welcome it.

This drawing in the usual convulsive style of Virgil Partch appeared in the *Wall Street Journal*.

STRATEGIC LOCATION? *The right site can put you in a commanding position in your industry. Columbus and Southern site selectors can find you the right spot for a plant — and keep it completely confidential. In fact, Columbus and Southern owns many sites you may wish to consider.* © McCann-Marschalk Co., Inc.

Cartoonist Charles E. Slackman did this ad as one in a series for "Sanforized."

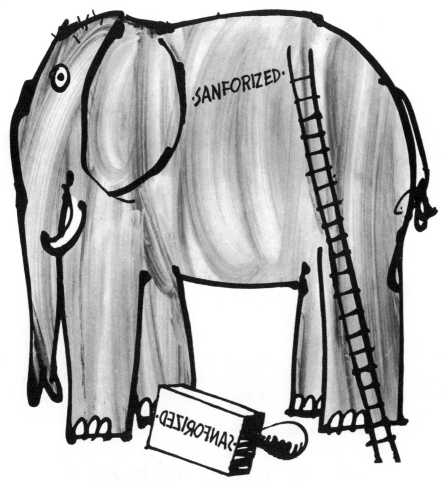

If it meets our standards...

Courtesy Cluett, Peabody Co., Inc.

Art Director Alan H. Zwiebel of Young and Rubicam says:

"In a field dominated by photographers, the appropriate use of the cartoon can be an effective way of establishing a fresh graphic look to an advertisement or a campaign.

"More important, the cartoon can succeed as an illustration in situations where a photograph would either be impractical, unachievable or inappropriate.

"The one common denominator in all these cartoons is the freshness of style that sets them apart from other kinds of illustration. This 'freshness' is most important when approaching art directors in the advertising field."

"The Shame!
My son flunking
Bartender School
for not using
Angostura in Manhattans!"

Two more drawings by "Vip" for the classic, long-running campaign by Angostura Aromatic Bitters.

Courtesy Angostura-Wupperman Corp.

"Him? He made an Old Fashioned and forgot the Angostura!"

According to Herb Valen, former gag man, now head of Valen Associates, a cartoonists' talent agency: "Cartoon advertising is being used by more agencies than ever before to get their clients' messages across to the public. Market surveys show that cartoon advertising has consistently high readership; and puts the readers in a good, receptive (buying) frame of mind."

Cook like a "PRO"!

Simple-style cartoon like this one gets the message across with good humor and effectiveness—*and sticks in one's memory!*

Courtesy of the Florida Natural Gas Association

90% OF ALL RESTAURANT FOOD is cooked with gas. Because professional chefs *know* that their reputations . . . their very jobs . . . depend on *results*. So what's in it for *you?* Just this:

Inevitably, when it is a big-name client and the campaign has been planned by a big-name agency, a big-name cartoonist will be used. After all, the client can pay. Why shouldn't he identify with someone whose work is immediately recognizable to millions of newspaper and magazine readers?

The "name cartoonist," then, does not have to go out looking for advertising work. It pursues him at home, on the golf course, in the steam room—even out on his boat. There is no escape for the poor fellow. He just can't get away from those fat checks.

Courtesy Dow Corning Corp.

This cartoon illustration by B. Wiseman certainly puts across the name of the product in a lively, amusing way.

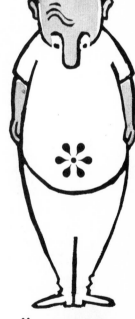

UNCERTAIN STOMACH

When your stomach feels uncertain from indigestion, heartburn, gas pains, nausea or other symptoms of excess acidity, remember this: **Each small PHILLIPS' TABLET consumes 37%**

Here's a very funny advertising cartoon that pinpoints exactly where the trouble spot is.

Courtesy Phillips' Tablets

Small wonder this adulation of big names among advertisers! Who will ever forget that great series of long ago by Dr. Suess for an insect repellent company in which the slogan became practically a household expression, "Quick, Henry—the Flit!" Or more recently a long-running campaign by Richard Decker that needed no blurb beyond, "In Philadelphia nearly everybody reads the Bulletin?"

If you don't know the leading business publication, look for this symbol.

If an industry doesn't have a business publication, it's probably not legal.

If it does have a business publication, you'll find that its pages are the fastest way to learn what's new, how-to, and who's who. And if you keep reading the business press, you'll learn that some publications are better than others. More often than not the leaders will be flying the ABP symbol from their mastheads.

Courtesy American Business Press, Inc.

The art of William Steig has graced innumerable prize-winning campaigns.

Take
a moment

Take
a moment

for Murine

Great attention-getters were these two ads by famous cartoonist Whitney Darrow, Jr., part of a series.

for Murine

...drive in
comfort!

Courtesy the Murine Co., Inc.

...wake up
faster!

The author got an extra lift, too, when he received the check for this drawing.

Courtesy Beminal 817

Give your patient that extra lift with "Beminal" 817

Even in an ad the great George Price's work never fails to bring an instant smile, as it does here.

Courtesy N. W. Ayer &
Son, Inc., for electric
companies advertising program

Scouting for facts?

Most people know that their electric service comes from a business owned by investors—owned by thousands of <u>people</u> like you and your neighbors. It does <u>not</u> come from government—not the city, not the state. Do <u>you</u> know it, too?

(COMPANY SIGNATURE)

But what about the lesser-known, or completely "unknown" cartoonist. What chance does *he* have of selling his work to an advertising agency and having it featured in a great, glamorous, money-making campaign?

Here, again, the answer is similar to the situation at magazines and newspapers. The insecurity of accounts brought about by the rating system, among other things, keeps agencies on their toes, guaranteeing the chances of virgin talent crashing through. Art directors can ill afford not to be on the alert at all times, ready, willing, and anxious to explore every new portfolio that comes along in the hopes of finding an innovation in comic art

Cartoon by Don Madden, courtesy of the Exercycle Corp.

Funny, it wasn't there last summer.

**Bringing the kids?
Let Hilton worry about it**

"Childlike" style used in this ad reveals sound knowledge of drawing on closer inspection.

Courtesy Hilton Hotels Corp.

How can you get your work seen by these art directors? One way might be to go directly to the advertising agency and try to get past the reception desk. But sad to say, you might find yourself running smack into a brick wall attempting this because receptionists sometimes have a way of not being receptive. Or, if you did succeed in getting past her (they generally are feminine) and managed to snare the art director, you might only alienate the poor guy forever because he really was too busy to see you!

A better way would be to phone the agency and ask to speak to the art director. Perhaps he, or his secretary, will give you an appointment. Or perhaps they will suggest that you drop off your portfolio and leave it for a few days. Agencies frequently exhibit the work of new artists in their offices so that account executives may see it and perhaps get stimulating new ideas for campaigns.

The probability, in any case, is that you will be treated with courtesy and respect.

Immediately identifiable is the smart sophisticated style of magazine and advertising cartoonist Charles Saxon.

American doesn't care <u>what</u> your baggage weighs.

These three were part of a long-running series done by me.

(The author has no scruples. He refuses to answer when people inquire what happened to *his* hair!)

Courtesy Fitch Shampoo

One final word about soliciting advertising work: Generally speaking it's a waste of time and just plain silly for you to try planning a whole campaign yourself. This job is best left to trained copy writers and other specialists. If you go dashing into an agency proclaiming that you have singlehandedly worked out a brand new slogan for a cigarette or beer client, and have done all the cartoons to boot, the chances are you won't even get a pat on the head for your trouble. At best you will merely be asked to sign a "release" before you go any further. This is the way agencies are forced to protect themselves in case you decide to start yelling "plagiarism" later.

Leave the problems of dreaming up new advertising campaigns to those other fellows and concentrate on selling yourself as a cartoonist. Prepare nice samples of your best work, phone for that appointment—and sally forth!

10. HOW TO SELL A COMIC STRIP

Ah, the comic strips! Excuse me while I brush away a tear or two. I was weaned on the funnies and like all children with a penchant for drawing, spent nearly all my time copying my favorites. Indeed, to this day I can still draw some of them fairly accurately, I believe. Here, look—

Do you think I retained the influence of any of these childhood gods of mine? If so, all I can say is I'm deeply grateful and wish only that I could have repaid them some of the many happy hours they gave me—and millions of others.

The dream of nearly every free-lance cartoonist is to sell a comic strip. Here he sees himself with an audience of maybe a hundred million readers. If he has luck the movies or television will adapt his property. He will become rich and famous. What nicer way is there to seek fame and fortune?

Comic strips began roughly about 1896 with "The Yellow Kid" by Outcault. As a result of circulation wars among newspapers, the success of this feature swiftly led to the inauguration of others. By the early 1900's we had Dirks' Katzenjammer Kids, Opper's Happy Hooligan, Schultze's Foxy Grandpa, McCay's Little Nemo, Fisher's Mutt and Jeff, Tad's Outdoor and Indoor Sports, Kahles' Hairbreadth Harry, Hershfield's Abie the Agent, Sterrett's Polly and Her Pals, McManus' The Newlyweds (later Bringing Up Father), and a raft of panel ideas by Rube Goldberg culminating in Boob McNutt.

The mid-twenties raised the curtain on many other immortals— Carl Ed's Harold Teen, Frank King's Gasoline Alley, Harold Gray's Little Orphan Annie, Jimmy Murphy's Toots and Casper, Billy de Beck's Barney Google, Elzie Segar's Thimble Theatre (Popeye), George Herriman's Krazy Kat, and Walter Hoban's Jerry on the Job.

That golden age of comics also saw the birth of The Nebbs, Smitty, Just Kids, Reg'lar Fellers, Winnie Winkle, Tillie the Toiler, Ella Cinders, Fritzi Ritz, Dick Tracy, and Joe Jinks. In 1926 Ham Fisher came up with Joe Palooka, followed later by Al Capp's L'il Abner, Chester Gould's Dick Tracy, Milt Caniff's Terry and the Pirates (he later switched to Steve Canyon), and . . . oops! we nearly left out James Swinnerton, Milt Gross, H. T. Webster, Clare Briggs, J. R. Williams, and many others too humorous to mention. Who will say that anyone ever won the heart of America more, or mirrored the times with deeper understanding and wisdom than these hallowed greats of our profession?

Krazy Kat   **by George Herriman**

© 1938 King Features Syndicate, Inc.

Historians of the comic strip never fail to mention George Herriman's great, poetic classic "Krazy Kat" which chronicled for over thirty years the love affair of a cat and a mouse, under the watchful (sometimes) eye of "Offissa Pupp."

Does a comic character stay the same once it is created? Not always, judging by Popeye, whose earnings from TV and assorted royalties have surpassed $20,000,000!

December, 1919. Debut of "Thimble Theatre." That's Olive Oyl at right.

January 17, 1929. First appearance of Popeye.

January 17, 1930, one year after Popeye's debut. The little man is Castor Oyl.

July 28, 1933. The delivery of Swee'pea.

The main problem in thinking up a comic strip, of course, is the central character. And whether you are planning an adventure strip or a gag strip, the prerequisites are the same. First, your hero must be capable of winning the sympathy of vast multitudes of readers who will adopt and take him to their collective breast. Second, like the rock of ages, he must be able to withstand the test of endless time and not wear out after a few short weeks or months.

Let's discuss that first prerequisite a bit further. Creating a character with whom readers will have strong sympathy does not necessarily mean that he must be an exemplary one. In fact, weakness in a character sometimes makes us love him all the more. For example, Schulz' little people in "Peanuts" frequently are mean and selfish in

their dealings with each other. But because we can "identify" with them, we understand them and therefore they are *funny*. The same is true of many of Al Capp's characters, Chic Young's, and others.

Now for the second prerequisite—durability. Obviously, if you try to interest a syndicate editor in the feasibility of a strip about a plumber, he's going to wonder what will happen after a few months of gags about leaky faucets and flooded basements. The same is true if you submit an adventure strip called, let's say, "Sven of the Ski Slopes," a story of a ski instructor. How long can you keep Sven on ice—or in splints—before readers start losing interest, the editor will be asking himself as he examines your samples?

I sound skeptical about such characters, yet years ago if Al Capp had described a strip based on a family with the kookey name of "Yokum" living in some swamp, I might have sounded the same. Or, more recently, had free-lance cartoonist Mort Walker sounded me out on a dumb army private named "Beetle Bailey," I might have advised him to go on contributing one-panel cartoons to magazines.

The syndicate editor buying comic strips and newspaper panels, has that responsibility, of deciding which features have a chance of gaining a lasting place for themselves in the affections of millions of readers who are already in love with the Blondies, Steve Canyons, L'il Abners, Peanuts, Dick Tracys, etc. He must be sure if he is amused or thrilled with the samples you are showing him, that you are no flash in the pan and can keep up the high standard of work necessary to hold clients. For make no mistake, there is no lifetime guarantee when newspapers take on a feature. They can, and will, cancel out when a cartoon falters or rival syndicates show them something better.

John Celardo demonstrates the wide range of the modern adventure strip cartoonist in "Tarzan," from the teeming jungle of Africa to a prize ring in New York City—all on one Sunday page!

One of the oldest of strips, done by its original creator, Rudy Dirks, and now carried on by his artist son John! These lovable brats, of course, set the style for countless "Kartoon Kids" that followed.

© 1965 by United Feature Syndicate, Inc.

Prankish and unpredictable, small fry are just naturally good subjects for the cartoonist. So, next time one practices saxophone next door or skates noisily by on your sidewalk, don't start hollering. Study him!

Some immortals in this field well-worth digging into the archives for, are Frank Swinnerton's "Little Jimmy," Ad Carter's "Just Boys," and Percy Crosby's "Skippy."

More modern greats are Carl Anderson's "Henry," Marge's "Little Lulu," and, of course, Hank Ketcham's "Dennis the Menace."

These typical daily strips from Chic Young's "Blondie" illustrate how the comic artist has made over a hundred million readers feel that they are all part of the Bumstead household, sharing its wonderful topsy-turvy world of excitement.

A never-ending stream of novel ideas, hilarious social satire, flamboyant drawing, sexy gals and muscle men, humor and humility—those are just a few of All Capp's patent ingredients for keeping "Li'l Abner" on top in the comic strip industry.

No single cartoonist has contributed more to raising the standards of comic strip art than the much imitated, super-talented Milt Caniff. This particular Sunday page, for example, travelers will attest is 100 per cent authentic Hong Kong!

STEVE'S NEW ORDERS READ — HONG KONG!

WHICH MEANS "ISLE OF FRAGRANT WATERS", BUT IT SPELLS EXCITEMENT IN ANY LANGUAGE IN THE WORLD...

FROM THE HARBOR AT NIGHT...

...TO THE TEEMING NATIVE QUARTER

FROM THE FERRY SLIPS...

...TO THE VIEW FROM THE RAIL AS THE SUZY WONGS DISPLAY THEIR OWN BRAND OF LOCAL SCENERY—TWICE A DAY AT THE COMMUTATION HOURS...

...AND THE NEW KAI TAK AIRPORT...

NEAR THE OLD STRIP WHICH WAS SO BEATEN UP BY BOTH SIDES IN WORLD WAR TWO...

IT IS HERE THAT STEVE'S FLIGHT SLIPS GRACEFULLY DOWN BETWEEN THE PEAKS...BUT THERE IS A COMMOTION AMONG THE WELCOMING PARTY...

'OP IT, ALF! THE RUDDY AIRCRAFT IS LANDING...

AND WE CAN'T FIND THE FLYING OFFICER'S LIP ROUGE!

New York-born Ernie Bushmiller started "Fritzi Ritz" in 1922, but it wasn't until fifteen years later that he introduced her niece "Nancy" in a strip of her own. Extremely simple style contributes greatly to this feature's enormous popularity.

From the drawing board of Alfred Andriola comes an example
of how he constructs one of his typical "Kerry Drake" strips.

1. Andriola prepares a basic "rough".

2. He advances to a comprehensive pencil drawing.

A finished "Kerry Drake" looks like this—

Kerry Drake   **by Alfred Andriola**

Al Andriola says:

"How do you set down in words the process for drawing a comic strip? After twenty-five years, it's like shaving—a habit that one is accustomed to, yet is individual with each man, whether he is shaving or drawing.

"The idea must come first, obviously. The story, the characters, the locale, the gimmicks, the names for the villains and the subsidiary cast—all must be decided in advance. Then the plot must be broken down into weeks, and the weeks into days, so that each strip progresses the action and yet in itself possesses a measure of unity—while it develops plot, suspense, humor or character traits.

"Once all that is accomplished, I do a *very* rough rough, one which never leaves my studio, but I am allowing it to be published here. It is merely a breakdown, so that I can see how the whole week (six strips and a Sunday page) look, feel, move and build.

"From that the pencilling is drawn on Strathmore two-ply Bristol board. The finished strip is done over the pencilling, with crow quill pen points, sable brushes and Higgins black ink. Sometimes I apply Ben Day paper to areas that I want in a gray tone. That's all there is to it—but why, after all these years, does it still take so long to do? If you enjoy doing it, it's not a chore. After all, there are no short cuts, even to shaving, and if you try, you get nicked pretty badly."

The excitement engendered daily by powerful action artist Roy Crane in "Buz Sawyer" is calculated to leave readers of over 500 newspapers limp even before they have their morning coffee!

Buz Sawyer   **by Roy Crane**

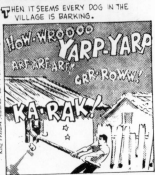

© 1965 King Features Syndicate, Inc.

You don't have to be a detective to track down clues to Chester Gould's success with his world-renowned "Dick Tracy." The suspense and human interest stand out like a small boy's fingerprints after he's raided the cookie jar.

Some guys have all the luck (and brains). Mort Walker not only does "Beetle Bailey"—

—he's also co-author of "Hi and Lois" with Dik Browne!

It is no secret that most successful newspaper cartoonists, on account of the pressure of all the work they must do, employ assistants, or "ghosts." One of the most successful of these is Bob Dunn, ex-president of the National Cartoonists Society, an organization that includes among its members almost every important name in the business. For years he was associated with Milt Gross in turning out the great daily cartoon, "That's My Pop!" Then, when Milt retired, the late Jimmy "They'll Do It Every Time" Hatlo was quick to take on the talented, adaptable Dunn.

Bob says: "Jimmy was a perfectionist, very demanding of his

helpers. But in all fairness, he was equally tough on himself. It was hard achieving 'neatness' after the wild style of Milt's drawings. But I liked 'They'll Do It Every Time' and stuck it out. It's a great feature —in 820 papers, along with 'Little Iodine' and 'Hatlo's History.'

"Assisting a star cartoonist is a good way to get into the business. A youngster should first learn to letter well. Then he must draw all the time—go to an accredited school. If he doesn't want to draw morning, noon, and night, it means he'd better see about getting into something else besides the insecure, difficult, wonderful world of the funnies."

Hear that, professional-cartoonist-to-be?

This little feature by Bil Keane, based exclusively on gags pertaining to television, enjoys deservedly wide distribution.

Channel Chuckles
By Bil Keane

"This town ain't big enough fer both of us."

Channel Chuckles
By Bil Keane

© 1965 Register-Tribune Syndicate, Inc.

The conquest of space means a race not only between nations but newspaper syndicates as well. In this one, "Our Space Age," Otto Binder's scientific writing is illustrated by a cartoonist highly skilled in technical drawing, Carl Pfeufer.

Our Space Age

...with

DR. FRONTIER

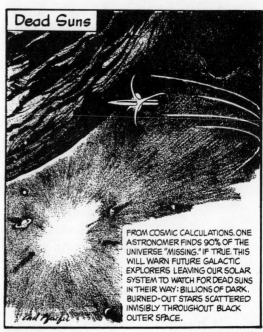

Dead Suns

FROM COSMIC CALCULATIONS, ONE ASTRONOMER FINDS 90% OF THE UNIVERSE "MISSING." IF TRUE, THIS WILL WARN FUTURE GALACTIC EXPLORERS LEAVING OUR SOLAR SYSTEM TO WATCH FOR DEAD SUNS IN THEIR WAY: BILLIONS OF DARK, BURNED-OUT STARS SCATTERED INVISIBLY THROUGHOUT BLACK OUTER SPACE.

SCIENCE *—not fiction—* **DRAMATIZED!**

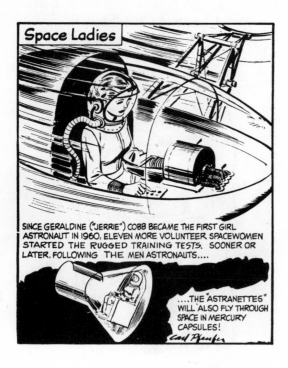

Space Ladies

SINCE GERALDINE ("JERRIE") COBB BECAME THE FIRST GIRL ASTRONAUT IN 1960, ELEVEN MORE VOLUNTEER SPACEWOMEN STARTED THE RUGGED TRAINING TESTS. SOONER OR LATER, FOLLOWING THE MEN ASTRONAUTS....

....THE "ASTRANETTES" WILL ALSO FLY THROUGH SPACE IN MERCURY CAPSULES!

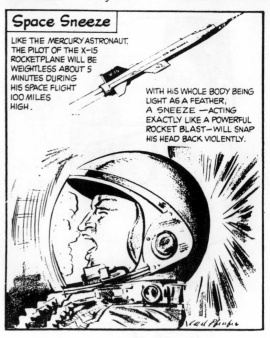

Space Sneeze

LIKE THE MERCURY ASTRONAUT, THE PILOT OF THE X-15 ROCKETPLANE WILL BE WEIGHTLESS ABOUT 5 MINUTES DURING HIS SPACE FLIGHT 100 MILES HIGH.

WITH HIS WHOLE BODY BEING LIGHT AS A FEATHER, A SNEEZE —ACTING EXACTLY LIKE A POWERFUL ROCKET BLAST—WILL SNAP HIS HEAD BACK VIOLENTLY.

Syndicates keep trying to sell new strips. For instance, "The Good Old Days" by Erwin Hess specializes in nostalgic pen and ink drawings—

This daily cartoon feature is the first truly integrated comic strip. Its creator is a former member of the all-black 477th Bomber Group of the U.S. Air Force in World War II.

Turner also served with the Oakland (Calif.) Police Department, and his strip premiered in the *Berkeley Post*, a weekly newspaper for the black community.

"Wayout" by Ken Muse is—well, it's way out. . . .

Wayout   **by Ken Muse**

Fred Lasswell's rambunctious "Snuffy Smith" and his mountain-folk buddies—cartooning in the great tradition, and refreshing as a swig o' corn likker!

Barney Google and Snuffy Smith • by Fred Lasswell

Major domo at King Features Syndicate is editor Sylvan Byck who says:

"There is no formula for a successful comic strip. Strips that seemed unpromising at the start have scored smash hits and others that appeared to have all the earmarks of success have failed to make the grade.

"However, there are some things I always look for in a new strip, and it is possible to point out a few guidelines that may be helpful to the cartoonist whose aim is syndication.

"The most important ingredients in a comic strip, in my opinion, are the warmth and charm of its central characters. If it is a humor strip, readers must like the characters enough to laugh *with* them as well as *at* them. If it is a narrative strip, readers must care enough about the hero to really want him to win out over the villain.

"An artist who attempts to create a comic strip character is in effect trying to create the equivalent of a movie or TV star. If you will stop and think about it a minute, you will see why this is so. When Bob Hope steps into view on the TV tube, all of us are on his side immediately. We *want* to laugh at his jokes because his charm and the warmth of his personality make us like him. With only his pen to aid him, the cartoonist is faced with the task of bringing to "life" a personality that, hopefully, will match that of a Bob Hope or a Cary Grant or a Red Skelton. It isn't easy, but the rewards are substantial for those who can do it.

"Although characterization is the most important element of a comic, the cartoonist also must cope with the problem of choosing a theme for his new strip. What will it be about?

"Actually, it is possible to do a successful comic strip about almost anything or anybody if the writing and drawing are exactly right for the chosen subject. In general, though, it is best to stay away from themes that are too confining. If you achieve your goal of syndication, you want your strip to last a long time. You don't want to run out of ideas after a few weeks or months.

"In humor strips, it is better to build around a character than around a job. For example, it is possible to do some very funny comic strip gags about a taxi driver. But a strip that is limited to taxi driver gags is bound to wear thin pretty fast. I'd rather see a strip about a warmly funny man who just happens to earn his living as a cabbie, and whose job is only a minor facet of his potential for inspiring gags.

"Narrative strips can be and often are based on the central character's job. For example, the basis of a private eye strip is the work he does. But even here the strip will only be as successful as the characterization in it. The big question is what *kind* of a man is this particular private eye.

"A few final words. Syndication is the big leagues. A young sandlot outfielder would hardly think of applying for Mickey Mantle's job without first getting some minor league experience. Learn how to draw. Learn how to write. Keep at it until your work has the polish of a professional.

"Then, and only then, produce a set of samples and submit them to the syndicates.

"Good luck!"

Rags-to-riches success story of Charles M. Schulz is an inspiration to all unknown cartoonists. In 1949 the struggling young Minneapolitan timidly mailed a package of drawings to a New York City syndicate, then waited breathlessly with his wife to learn how they had been received.

Snoopy, here shown in one of Charles Schulz' great daily strips "Peanuts," threatens to become the most renowned dog in all cartoon history.

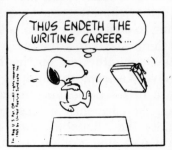

And so, dear young cartoonist, there they are—the best in the business. If you are going to try a newspaper strip or panel, don't just read them, STUDY them! Learn from all these contemporary masters what you should, or should not, do. For example, if you are not a skilled draftsman like Milt Caniff, Roy Crane, or John Celardo, don't try to compete with them—at least not until you have carried your study of art much further. The best story line or scenario won't help if your drawings are crude and amateurish. On the other hand if your style of drawing is serious, or even semi-serious, do not try to make it comical, like Ernie Bushmiller, Charlie Schulz, Al Capp, or Fred Lasswell.

Figure out your qualifications, then prepare samples—avoiding sophisticated or controversial subjects. Remember, this is for newspapers! And don't be afraid to submit your work to the syndicates. Remember that Charlie Schulz might still be working for "peanuts," instead of having them work for him, if he had been afraid!

11. POLITICAL CARTOONING

Cartooning is a funny business but when it comes to the editorial page there is no kidding around. The cartoon is found here by virtue of the ancient maxim that "one picture is worth a thousand words." Newspaper editors know the reluctance on the part of readers to wade through monotonous columns of print—hence, the political cartoon. Typography keeps improving all the time but it still hasn't been able to take the place of a drawing!

All cartoons are, in a way, a mirror of the times but the political cartoon is most exclusively that. A study of this Republic since it was founded shows that engravings based on current topics were most instrumental in shaping the course of policy and politics. The pen, indeed, is mightier than the sword—especially when dipped in India ink!

Many social reforms that we enjoy today were instigated originally by political cartoons.

Here Jim Ivey sees the Republican Party pondering its identity.

"WHO AM I?"   © The San Francisco Examiner

Various causes such as Child Labor, The Eight-Hour Day, Women's Suffrage, Trust Busting, and Free Education began right on the drawing boards of men like Kemble, Sullivant, Davenport, Opper, McCutcheon, T. E. Powers, and Art Young whose graphic portrayals of existing evils aroused a lethargic public to press their legislators for action. The symbol of Prohibition, a gaunt undertaker with an umbrella, invented by Rollin Kirby, did much to destroy the 18th Amendment. And further back, in the nineteenth century, it was Thomas Nast whose drawings slew Boss Tweed and ended the political corruption of that era. "Political cartoons can break my bones, but names can never harm me," Tweed might have parodied in those days. Many another Goliath of corruption has been felled by a political cartoonist's slingshot.

In the hands of a capable craftsman, the political cartoon is a most effective weapon of propaganda. Whom he loves, walks in beauty. Whom he hates, is likened to the lowliest denizen of the underbrush.

Hell hath no fury like a political cartoonist!

Requirements: Must have great skill as an artist. Drawings must frequently contain simple dignity on some days, as well as blistering irony on others. Must maintain an up-to-the-minute grasp of local, state, and world affairs. Must possess talent for caricature since likenesses are so often called for. Must have sense of humor that can be translated into politics.

Below, political cartoonist Fischetti takes note of a "split" between the Soviet Union and Red China.

Fischetti

© 1965 New York Herald Tribune, Inc.

"WE HAVE A LOT IN COMMON....SHE LOATHES MY WORK AND I ABHOR HERS"

Symbols are the stock in trade of the political cartoonist. Nast invented the tiger as the representative of Tammany. I already mentioned Kirby's undertaker. Will Johnstone invented a naked taxpayer clad only in a barrel. If you can invent symbols, so much the better. Here are some others which are standard equipment for the political cartoonist:

Uncle Sam

Uncle Sam can also be a woman. Here she is cleaning house. (The dust could be labeled "dirty politics," "illegal lotteries," etc.)

Peace is always a beautiful dame. (Highly desirable—maybe that's why.)

Ol' Man Mars is still playing his part although he wouldn't last a second in modern warfare in this get up.

The Republican & Democratic Parties carry on.

LABOR looks like this on the editorial pages. (Except when it's "racketeer controlled.")

Free Enterprise. Ancient delineations of the fat capitalist have changed to this.

SOME HANDY CLICHÉS

This picture is called "Stamping Him Out." Him can be Crime, Bossism, TAXES or Unpreparedness—provided the foot belongs to Uncle Sam or a reasonable facsimile. On the other hand, the foot can be the "villain" marked "Racketeering" in which case the fellow on the floor is labeled "Inadequate Police, The Law," etc.

Here is "The Rising Tide," usually Public Indignation about to drown out Butch Caponi, Public Enemy No. 1. The bolt of lightning might be the new Crime Commission appointed by the Governor.

Like a baseball pitcher, the political cartoonist sometimes uses a change of pace. He may alternate the seriousness of his work with drawings about Mother's Day, July Fourth, March of Dimes, Safety in Auto Driving, etc.

Political cartoonists' views of necessity have to coincide with that of their papers. If you worked for one paper, this is how your cartoon might look when the McGoof Bill on Armaments passed the House.

Here is what your cartoon might look like if you worked for a different paper.

Great Britain's Giles gives us a glance "Over There."

"I think we've satisfied her there are no bombs or hijackers on board, all she wants now is a guarantee she won't be tarred and feathered between here and Calais."

© London Daily Express

Commercialism on a holy day arouses Auth's ire in this drawing.

There will be six hours of football on television Christmas Day.

—News Item

© Philadelphia Inquirer

These two thought-provoking political cartoons are by Pulitzer prizewinner Bill Mauldin.

"HOLD 'EM BACK AT ALL COSTS, SPIRO!"

© The Chicago Sun-Times

"THIS IS ONLY A SIDELINE. MY MAIN INTEREST IS DOMESTIC POLICY."   © The Chicago Sun-Times

The Christian Science Monitor's LePelley illustrates "There Was an Old Lady Who Lived in a Shoe."

© The Christian Science Monitor

The *Daily Oklahoman*'s Lange gives youth this message on drugs, entitled "Travel Agency."

© The Daily Oklahoman

© The Knoxville Journal

Charlie Daniel vents his spleen on election matters.

Another Pulitzer prizewinner is C. D. Batchelor, political cartoonist of the newspaper with the largest paid circulation in the United States—the New York *Daily News*.

Here is a brilliant cartoon by young Don Wright.

Eclipse   © The Miami News

"You Don't Understand, Boy — You're Supposed To
Just Shuffle Along"

In these three pictures
Pulitzer prizewinner "Herblock"
passes judgment on civil rights,
medicare, and voting apport-
ionment.

Animal Farm

"Quick — Boil Lots Of Water"

from *Straight Herblock* (Simon & Schuster, 1964)

Since politics is highly partisan, you're either on one side or the other. It is impossible for the political cartoonist to make everybody happy with his work. If you agree with his point of view you will think he is very highly gifted. If you disagree with him, you will think he has no talent at all. Everybody can love a comic strip artist. Not everybody can love a political cartoonist. If you want to be loved by everybody, don't become a political cartoonist. No easy job his. A Dale Carnegie in reverse, he influences people and loses friends!

Giants of the past and present worth studying are: Fitzpatrick, Low, McCutcheon, Opper, Daumier, Talburt, T. E. Powers, Rollin Kirby and Duffy.

Below, Bill Sanders takes a stand on racial matters.

"I THOUGHT YOU SAID THE WORLD WOULD COME TO AN END, DADDY!"

As you have seen, most political cartoonists are adept draftsmen, letterers, and caricaturists. If this is your chosen field, sharpen up your talents in all these departments—especially the last. If called upon to draw the likeness of some famous personage, it is extremely doubtful that any editor will give you a month to do it.

Practice summarizing daily news events with one single drawing. Spring these on your friends. When they start saying, "Gee! That's awfully good!" take a few samples to your local newspaper office and see if the editor says the same thing.

Oh, yes—be sure to pick a paper that agrees with the sentiments expressed in your drawings. Otherwise, you might not get much encouragement.

In this cartoon Don Dowling was inspired by thoughts of a holocaust.

Twenty Years After

Crime on the home front draws fire from crusading editorial cartoonist Gene Basset.

"BUON GIORNO, GIOVANNI... HOW'S BUSINESS?"

© Scripps-Howard Newspapers

Tony Auth makes a desperate plea for the Emerald Isle.

© Philadelphia Inquirer

Jim Lange takes a disquieting view of us at sea.

© The Daily Oklahoman

A million readers *get the picture* on ecology and the "youth problem" from L. D. Warren.

SILENT SPRING

'WONDER WHAT'S WRONG WITH KIDS TODAY? BRING ME AN ASPIRIN, WILL YOU, DEAR?'

© Los Angeles Times Syndicate

Tom Darcy, too, has a thought on the environment.

© Los Angeles Times Syndicate

'REMEMBER THE GOOD OLD DAYS WHEN YOU USED A SHELL TO HEAR THE OCEAN'S ROAR?'

Heads of government are putty in the hands of political cartoonists, and the President of the United States is no exception.

Here he finds a facsimile of himself on one end of an elephant, placed there by Roy Peterson.

"Things may look bad to some students of international affairs—however we are constantly in the process of re-evaluating our perspective of Canadian-American relations..."

Then, undiscouraged, up he pops on a table of cartoonist Paul Szep's, along with the "veep" and another dignitary.

"...AND SPIRO BROUGHT THE BALL"

Here Doug Marlette has visions of an oncoming election promise.

"YOU KNOW IT AND I KNOW IT, BUT DOES **HE** KNOW IT?!"

Warren King chides an unsuccessful candidate in the Democratic primaries, as he returns to City Hall.

No sacred cow is safe from the God-unfearing wrath of political cartoonist Pat Oliphant. In this picture, he attacks a Federal agency supposedly in existence to protect consumers—

GREAT MOMENTS IN RETAILING

—and in this one, Oliphant swings his brush at a mighty cartel allegedly enjoying certain privileges denied the majority.

'NEXT!'

Tom Engelhardt draws a cartoon about the same oligarchy's connections in high government places—*and tells us how he does it!*

© St. Louis Post-Dispatch

Open For Business

"I begin my day by checking out the latest news bulletins and determining which item demands an instant comment from me. Then I work up a 'rough' and show it to my editor. Occasionally, we will make changes and sometimes after those sessions, if the idea still doesn't come across, it's back to the ol' drawing board. At last, after all the wrinkles have been ironed out and I have the go-ahead, I proceed to make my finished drawing. In my opinion, it's impossible for any political cartoonist to work if his thoughts differ drastically from the policies of his paper. This does not mean minor issues, but certainly there must be harmony on the major ones—war, peace, civil rights, etc."

Does he ever receive threats on account of his work? Tom chuckled, "Yes, but thankfully, thus far there's been no actual violence. Once, during the hassle over Medicare, a lady who described herself as the wife of a doctor called up and said if she had a 'gun she'd shoot me. Happily, nothing ever came of it, unless that lady did get a gun and shoot herself with it accidentally, instead."

Englehardt laughingly boasts that though some of his colleagues have suffered broken homes over a political cartoon they did, his is still intact.

ONE. Tom Engelhardt doodles a "rough."

'I FOUND A POT OF GOLD AT THE END OF A RED, WHITE AND BLUE RAINBOW'

TWO. He carries his sketch a bit further.

THREE. Editorial approval having been obtained, he does the finish!

ENGELHARDT © St. Louis Post-Dispatch

'I Found A Pot Of Gold At The End Of A Red, White and Blue Rainbow'

How many of these personalities can you identify from the pen
of outstanding caricaturist and political cartoonist Ranan Lurie?

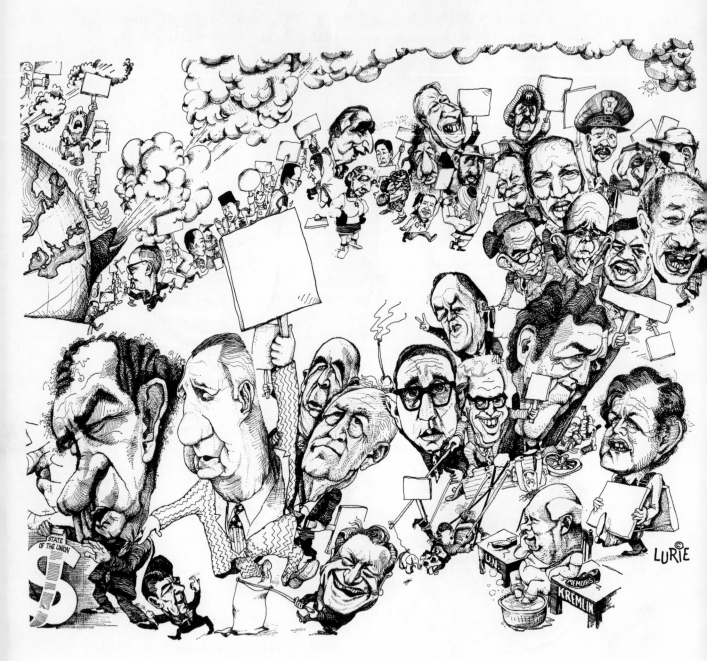

© Lurie, in Life

12. THE CARTOON AS ILLUSTRATION FOR CHILDREN'S STORIES

Sir John Tenniel's drawings for *Alice's Adventures in Wonderland*, though done over a hundred years ago, continue to rival Lewis Carroll's text in popularity among readers of all ages.

It was inevitable that children's book illustrators achieve this high niche. Youngsters love pictures, and the quality of work in the profession has improved steadily. Don't we immediately conjure a Dr. Seuss drawing the instant we think of his text for *The Cat in the Hat?*

"Alice" by Sir John Tenniel.

The Cat in the Hat by Dr. Seuss.

© 1957 by Dr. Seuss

Illustration by Susan Perl for *Sharp and Shiny.*

McGraw-Hill

In all these books there is a perfect blend of two art forms—drawing and writing. Susan Perl couldn't possibly have done justice to Lewis Carroll; it would have been a mistake for Dr. Seuss (or Herriman) to try illustrating *Sharp and Shiny*, and had Sir John tried fitting onto a page with *The Cat in the Hat*, he probably never would have been knighted.

Drawing from my book
The Litter Knight.

McGraw-Hill

The "marriage broker" in this union of artist and writer is, of course, the editor. One of the most important of these is Charlotte Zolotow, of Harper & Row, herself the author of dozens of children's books. What does she look for in an illustrator? "It's so hard to pin down because any artist who is really getting some of himself on the page is doing what only he can do, and that makes it good. Let's say we look for warmth and humor and feeling and the suitability of the picture to the words. A good illustration is an interpretive kind of art which contributes an extra dimension beyond the words themselves. For instance, if the author says it is early morning in the park and the illustrator shows someone walking past an empty trash basket, and the author goes on to evening in the park and the illustrator shows the trash basket overflowing, *that* is an extra dimension—especially if the author didn't mention trash baskets at all."

Beginner Books, a division of Random House, Inc., is the home base of Ted Geisel ("Dr. Seuss"), author of *The Cat in the Hat* as well as dozens of other works, and unquestionably the most widely acclaimed of all children's book writer-artists. Editor Michael K. Frith has this advice for those who would wander into his office with portfolios of their work:

"First of all, the illustrator must be able to *draw well,* a basic but seemingly oft-ignored requirement in children's books. This does not mean that he has to be able to draw *accurately* (Seuss's cat does not look any more like a cat than Walt Kelly's Pogo looks like a 'possum—we simply accept that they are what we're told they are —and both are marvelously *drawn*) but that he has to draw with *conviction.* With this it is essential that he have a very highly developed design sense . . . our pages are carefully balanced between picture and text, and particularly in the books for beginning readers this balance becomes crucial. The illustrator cannot afford to ignore or overpower the text he is illustrating.

"As for style, the most important aspect is originality. We're innately distrustful of the people who are peddled as being able to 'give you whatever you want.' Most such art is pretty hollow and usually pretty transitory, stylish but with neither life nor longevity. So we never look to follow the quirks of the current vogue but much prefer to explore the individualism of a particular illustrator.

"Finally, most important, and least definable of all, is a quality which I don't think anyone can manufacture, an ingredient which all the great illustrators have, a kind of left-over childishness that allows them to see things with a child's perception. By combining this with their sophisticated skills, they communicate directly and powerfully with children. Unfortunately, many illustrators seem more intent on communicating with art directors (the raw-color-with-no-outline school), with greeting card manufacturers (the funny-little-cross-eyed-men-with-bulbous-noses school), or with other adults who have a misty and most unrealistic nostalgia for the 'Kind of Book that I Liked when I Was a Child' (the fuzzy-mouse school). These books proliferate, often accompanied by the most overwhelming flackery and much media excitement, and die. And left behind are the books that the children like."

This is the Spanish edition of my book, *Danny and the Dinosaur.*

Harper & Row

Steven Kellogg gives a perfect demonstration of giving a story an extra lift in this drawing.

Pathos and high adventure are dexterously portrayed in all the young illustrator's work for Miriam T. Young's *Can't You Pretend?*

G. P. Putnam's Sons

Man's best friend (except when he is off the leash, perhaps) runs rampant in children's books, naturally.

Simon & Schuster

This story, by the well-known animation film designer Mitchell Rose, is about a dog who becomes so famous he appears in Carnegie Hall, as well as on TV and the covers of magazines, and people beg him for his paw print.

The Tail That Wagged a Dog, by Robert Kraus.

Windmill Books

My own *super*-dachshund *Lengthy* (he never knew if the back of him was following the front!).

Virgil Partch's *Shaggy Fur Face*.

Windmill Books

G. P. Putnam's Sons

Drawing by Frank Asch for his book *The Blue Balloon*.

McGraw-Hill

Barbara Lucas, chief editor of children's books at G. P. Putnam, has something to say to the would-be illustrator, too. "My advice is to keep his drawings as simple as possible. Don't try everything at once. Study other artists' work, current and classic. Explain to yourself why, in your opinion, their work succeeds or fails. Try to develop your own individual style, but don't be discouraged if you realize that in the beginning it is heavily influenced by other artists' work. One often learns by imitation, but it should be only the foundation from which your own style grows. Understanding how to use color—to make it serve your style, not hamper it—is extremely important. And understanding as much as possible about color reproduction and how to do your own color plate separations well is vital to the professional illustrator."

Has the shrewd Miss Lucas ever been disappointed in an illustrator's work? "Yes, one brought in his black line drawings and they were so lovely they took my breath away. His color overlays seemed harmless enough until I saw the proof run. The color completely dominated—not in shade or intensity but in the way he had used it. The viewer's eye hardly noticed the beautiful fine line and *its* shading and detail. The great globs of color caught the eye and held it fast."

Putnam's editor concludes by saying, "I also recommend to a new illustrator that he do drawings for a complete story and put it into dummy form before taking his portfolio around for viewing. For it's very important to an editor to know how well and if he can *interpret* a story as well. The illustrations don't have to be finished ones, but his intentions for the finished product should be clear, including his notions about choice and numbers of color."

Harcourt Brace Jovanovich, Inc.

Even a house seems funny, as drawn by James Flora for his book *My Friend Charlie*.

Dorothy Briley, managing editor of books for younger readers at J. B. Lippincott, echoes the sentiments of Miss Lucas. She says, "We look for freshness, appeal, and originality in artists' work, coupled with skill and knowledge of the illustrating craft. Too many artists do beautiful pictures that can be reproduced only by the most expensive means. It is also important that an artist be able to sustain characterization throughout a book, revealing the characters' many moods, yet leaving no doubt about who is who from page to page. If we're lucky enough to find all that in an artist, it's an extra bonus to have him be faithful and reliable about deadlines—especially the ones involving revisions which are always needed yesterday."

More drawings by James Flora for *My Friend Charlie*.

Harcourt Brace Jovanovich, Inc.

This cow from another Flora book, *The Joking Man*, might not be able to give milk, but it certainly can give laughs!

Janet D. Chenery, Executive Editor of Children's Books at Simon & Schuster, chimes in with her conception of an artist: "What we look for in children's book illustrators is a variety of interests and ways of expressing the interests—an understanding of the subject to be illustrated, of stories, of children, and of the appropriateness of artwork to the story or given situation. We look for warmth, clarity (sometimes this means realism, but not necessarily), humor, and, of course, a degree of professional attitude which allows working together most easily. We look for artists who understand the restrictions of production, who have the ability to make separations for color work, who stay within one or two sizes of what finished artwork should be, who present clean art carefully done (especially when there are overlays), and who are able to meet a schedule. All this is asking for a lot, but we ask for it, or at least we look for it."

Simon & Schuster

Someone Always Needs a Policeman, and writer-artist David Brown proves it in this amusing children's book.

Whitney Darrow Jr. presents three brazen young scofflaws in Marie Winn's *Shiver, Gobble, and Snore.*

Here's one of 'em who looks like he's just about had it.

Simon & Schuster

This is Page One of author Jan Wahl's *Lorenzo Bear & Company*, illustrated by Fernando Krahn, showing a perfect blending of story and pictures.

Lorenzo Bear
one shiny evening
gazed hard at the silver full moon above.
"If man can get there,
animal can too!" he
claimed. Therefore he decided
he would build the first animal rocket.

(Note how dramatic effect has been helped by an excellent page layout. Laying out a page is frequently the *artist's* job!)

Was the "blast-off" successful? Judge for yourself by the faces of Lorenzo and his friends.

G. P. Putnam's Sons

Author Felice Holman needed a picture of someone with a strange idiosyncrasy for *The Future of Hooper Toote*. And who should come floating into her life but well-known cartoonist and illustrator Gahan Wilson.

Charles Scribner's Sons

Harper & Row

The cartoonist's job, of course, is to "humanize" his animals. Here's how I handled it with *The Horse in Harry's Room*.

See how tame José Aruego's *Leo the Late Bloomer* is!

Windmill Books

How are children's books born? This one, according to its creators, "springs from the imaginative wit, the warmth, and the down-to-earth honesty of the native Philippine folklore."

A CROCODILE'S TALE
A Philippine Folk Story by
JOSE & ARIANE ARUEGO

Charles Scribner's Sons

In the drawing below, from his book *Look What I Can Do,* distinguished illustrator José Aruego reverses his usual position—or that of a bull.

Charles Scribner's Sons

Aruego insists that many of the animals in his books seem to resemble his best friends, in-laws, and other favorite people!

This is the "wrap-around" jacket of another bull story.

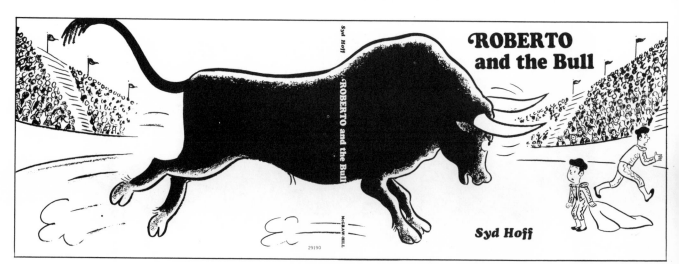

McGraw-Hill

Notice how the spine (center) contains the title, name of author and publisher, and does not interfere with any detail of the drawing.

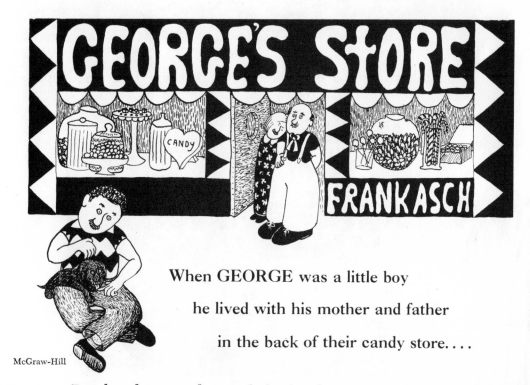

McGraw-Hill

When GEORGE was a little boy

he lived with his mother and father

in the back of their candy store....

People, places, and animals he has known provide the models, and much of the inspiration, for this author-artist's very funny first picture book—and Frank Asch begins his story right on the cover!

Don Madden demonstrates his skill at designing a cover/jacket that fits perfectly the mood of a book title.

Harcourt Brace Jovanovich, Inc.

It must have been a cold day in Miami when I dreamed up this one.

(Blood is thicker than water. Later I had to have my Eskimo character try his luck in the tropics.)

Holt, Rinehart and Winston, Inc.

Jack Kent offers evidence that a wolf in sheep's clothing can be funny, in his *Fables of Aesop*.

Parents' Magazine Press

Prolific Robert Kraus proves it even with bugs!

Oops! Here come comic-tycoons Mort Walker Dik Browne, making debut in children's ks, with *Most*.

Windmill Books

This charming pen-and-ink illustration is by Jacqueline Chwast, for *The Diary of a Paperboy*.

G. P. Putnam's Sons

Let us take a closer look at the talented team of Kent and Aesop.

This is "The Ass in the Lion's Skin," who taught us "You can get more respect by keeping your mouth shut."

Kent's drawing here is for "The Ox and the Frog." Moral: "Every windbag is punctured sooner or later."

Parents' Magazine Press

Here we have "Th and the Crow," illust the advice: "Don't be f by flattery."

"When you grasp a shadow, you lose the sub-stance," is of course the teaching of "The Dog and His Shadow."

Jack Kent doesn't need any help from Aesop to give us the greatest moral of all: IT PAYS TO KNOW HOW TO DRAW!

Somebody has a big appetite in this drawing by Gioia Fiammenghi from Lilian Moore's *Little Raccoon and No Trouble at All*.

A boy who envies the king of the jungle actually becomes a lion himself in my *Wilfred the Lion*.

A lion is even a doctor in this intriguing story for children, illustrated by Don Madden.

Perhaps since animals pop up so often in children's books, aspiring illustrators should patronize zoos and barnyards as diligently as they do art galleries.

An unidentified flying object by Garry Clark Hamilton for *Weeple People*.

McGraw-Hill

A sly fox and a hungry wolf are just part of the horde trying to devour *The Bun* in Marcia Brown's version of the Russian tale.

Charles Scribner's Sons

Cartoonist Don Madden kids us not about his cartooning in this illustration for Donald Burr's *Arithmetic for Billy Goats*.

Harcourt Brace Jovanovich, Inc.

For her deeply moving book, *The Life and Death of a Brave Bull*, Maia Wojciechowska naturally wanted an animal with strength and dignity, so famous war correspondent and illustrator John Groth filled the bill.

Harcourt Brace Jovanovich, Inc.

G. P. Putnam's Sons

These two animal drawings are from Robert Leydenfrost's *The Snake That Sneezed*.

Beasts lie down with lambs—and other animals—in children's books, as seen in this drawing by Roger Duvoisin for Louise Fatio's *The Happy Lion's Treasure.*

McGraw-Hill

This is Robert Leydenfrost's "Harold" who went around the jungle swallowing every creature he met—

—then continued on his merry way!

G. P. Putnam's Sons

I wonder how Harold would have made out had he encountered my own snake *Slithers,* who was "gentle even to the smallest worm."

G. P. Putnam's Sons

Can anyone deny the impact of Bugs Bunny and other cartoon film heroes on animal "art"? Here's Bugs in a typical action-filled sequence from one of his epic motion pictures.

Warner Bros. Productions

Another refugee from a vegetable patch, as seen by writer-artist Robert Kraus.

Wallace Tripp's mischievous pair set out to meet rabbits, or maybe even tigers, in *The Adventures of Mole and Troll* by Tony Johnson.

DADDY LONG EARS

BY ROBERT KRAUS

Windmill Books

G. P. Putnam's Sons

Sometimes writer-artists can't illustrate (or write) their own books!

Mark Stamaty had to do the drawings for Frank Asch's *Yellow! Yellow!*

McGraw-Hill

It was okay for me to illustrate my story *Where's Prancer?*—

Harper & Row

—but here I am, without my typewriter this time, illustrating Joan Lexau's great juvenile thriller *The Rooftop Mystery*.

Harper & Row

Mice are immensely popular among writers and artists, perhaps because they are the most consistent visitors to studios and garrets besides the rent collector. The first appearance of the great Mickey Mouse himself is said to have been an impromptu one, right on the drawing board of Walt Disney, way back in Kansas City before the Hollywood days.

Paul Galdone's drawings for the mouse books by Eve Titus have helped make Anatole (left) and Basil (right), here seen pursuing *The Pigmy Cats*, highly successful.

McGraw-Hill

My own *Baseball Mouse* goes after a sizzling line drive in this picture. (Having been born on a baseball field, it was only natural that he have big league aspirations.)

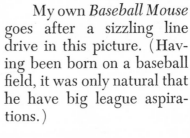

Famous cartoonist Eric Gurney did this drawing for his wife Nancy's tale *The King, the Mice, and the Cheese*.

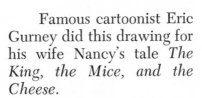

Random House

G. P. Putnam's Sons

Prolific Kraus, who went from *New Yorker* cartoonist to children's book author-illustrator to head of his own publishing company,

Windmill Books, says, "As a cartoonist I always drew pirates and various fairy tales, and I think the cartoonists that like that kind of thing probably can do children's books and those who deal with current events exclusively probably can't." He advised a seminar on children's books, conducted under the auspices of the Magazine Cartoonists Guild, as follows: "Do the best you can, give it everything you've got, do something you believe in, and, assuming what you believe in is correct, you'll be O.K."

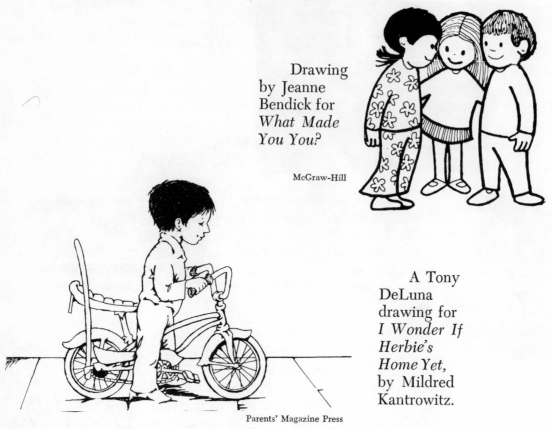

Drawing by Jeanne Bendick for *What Made You You?*

McGraw-Hill

A Tony DeLuna drawing for *I Wonder If Herbie's Home Yet,* by Mildred Kantrowitz.

Parents' Magazine Press

Children's book authors and illustrators make a valuable contribution to the peace of the world. They educate and entertain a generation that will take over tomorrow. They break down fears and superstitions. They eradicate borders and barriers, thus giving millions of little readers a feeling of solidarity and hope for the future.

If you love children and cherish them, try to become involved in this field. Fulfillment of the highest order awaits you, and if a steady flow of royalties rewards your efforts, you'll find that your cup truly runneth over.

13. HOW TO SURVIVE REJECTION SLIPS

""These are the times that try men's souls," said Thomas Paine during a critical period of this country's struggle for independence. And the poor cartoonist echoes this sentiment as his contributions come hurtling back from editorial offices accompanied by those nasty little missives called rejection slips. Even couched in the most delicate and tender language, their meaning adds up to about the same: "WE DON'T WANT YOU OR YOUR WORK. GET LOST."

What should the cartoonist do in trying times like these? There is a story about the late Hearst editor, Thomas Robertson, a gruff old codger, being accosted in his office by a would-be contributor. "You've been turning my stuff down for two years," the fellow complained. "How can I keep on going like this?"

"Eat sparingly," grunted old Robbie helplessly.

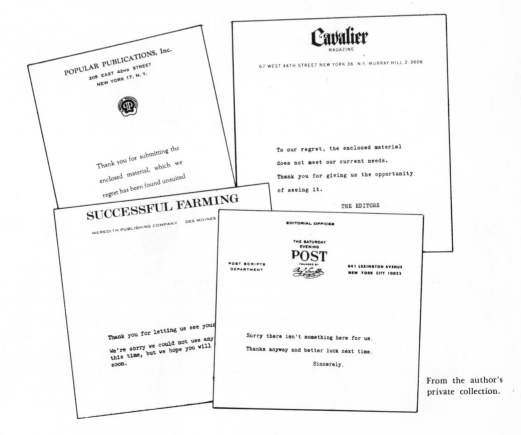

From the author's private collection.

Let us understand one thing: Editors do not enjoy rejecting contributors. The late Gurney Williams, of *Look,* once got nervous exhaustion after handing out 13,000 rejection slips in one afternoon; Jerry Beatty of *Esquire* put it off until he couldn't see over the top of his desk; Bob Schroeter of King Features has three secretaries who do it for him; Lawrence Lariar of *Parade* used to take contributors out for dinner first, until doctors warned him to cut down on his food intake. . . .

How about the poor recipients—the cartoonists? How do they feel? Lousy.

"In the early days I insulated my whole house in Great Neck with rejection slips," says Fred Neher.

"The first time I proposed I even got one from my wife," says George Price.

"Until I was twenty-eight they were the only things I ever read," says Robert Day.

Ned Hilton recalled that when he sold his first drawing he promptly moved out of his parent's house and rented an expensive studio. A month later he returned home with his suitcases because the rejection slips had started coming again. "For about five years I was the local business barometer, alternating between moving back and forth from home to a studio," said Ned.

Being rejected should not make you feel like shooting your brains out, or go dashing into the nearest tavern for a "quick one."

Nor should it make you feel like quitting. "Many a flower is born to blush unseen," said Thomas Gray, and many a great name in cartooning would never have become known if its owner gave up at first sign of a rejection slip. What a tragic loss it would be for you —and the whole world—if you could be the new Milton Caniff, Al Capp, or Peter Arno, and quit before you even got started!

The best thing to do until recognition comes is exactly what you are doing now. Until they became established Henry Boltinoff was a tennis pro, Al Kaufman helped dig the tunnel under New York's East River, Reamer Keller played cards on the Mississippi, and Phil Interlandi was a lifeguard at Laguna Beach. So, get off that bridge, or building ledge and—back to the old drawing board!

Society needs the cartoonist just as it needs the doctor, architect, and farmer. If you decide to make cartooning your profession, be proud—and tenacious, just like those other fellows.

What will the cartoon of the future be like? I don't know. Like all art forms I suppose it will change in one way or another. But one thing I'm certain of—it's here to stay.

So, dear reader, that's about all. I had intended asking the publishers to include a sheepskin diploma with this book—a sort of manifesto that you have satisfactorily completed this "Hoff Course in Cartooning." Then I figured that some might interpret a diploma as meaning their studies were concluded.

This is not the case! The pursuit of perfection in any art goes on and on. The best people in this profession are constantly striving to improve their work, never quite satisfied with what they have done. Every new picture must be better than the one before! The cartoonist who does not suffer this torment is suffering from conceit or stagnation.

But torment or not, the joy of giving birth to a picture is compensation enough—almost. I hope you pursue the Muse and one day come to share this feeling.

And now there is nothing left for me to do but close by wishing that your own "rejection slip period" is a not-too-long one, and that in all your future endeavors, be they cartooning or not, you receive many an

MARKETS

This is a partial list of the better-known magazines and syndicates that purchase cartoons. In addition to these, hundreds of other periodicals, ranging from trade organs to nationally popular magazines, use comic art on a regular or irregular basis. Since publications are forever dying and new ones are being born, it is suggested that you keep in touch with your local newsstand or public library for comprehensive, up-to-the-minute coverage.

American Legion
1345 Ave. of the Americas
New York, N.Y. 10019

Argosy
205 East 42nd Street
New York, N.Y. 10017

Better Homes & Gardens
1716 Locust Street
Des Moines, Iowa 50336

Boys' Life
Boy Scouts of America
New Brunswick, N.J. 08902

Cavalier
236 East 46th Street
New York, N.Y. 10017

Changing Times
1729 H Street, N.W.
Washington, D.C. 20006

Christian Science Monitor
1 Norway Street
Boston, Mass. 02115

Cosmopolitan
224 West 57th Street
New York, N.Y. 10019

Dude
236 East 46th Street
New York, N.Y. 10017

Family Circle
488 Madison Avenue
New York, N.Y. 10022

Gent
236 East 46th Street
New York, N.Y. 10017

Golf Digest
88 Scribner Avenue
Norwalk, Conn. 06856

Good Housekeeping
959 Eighth Avenue
New York, N.Y. 10019

King Features Syndicate
235 East 45th Street
New York, N.Y. 10017

Ladies' Home Journal
641 Lexington Avenue
New York, N.Y. 10022

McCall's Magazine
230 Park Avenue
New York, N.Y. 10017

McNaught Syndicate
60 East 42nd Street
New York, N.Y. 10017

Male
625 Madison Avenue
New York, N.Y. 10022

Man's Magazine
919 Third Avenue
New York, N.Y. 10022

Medical Economics
Kinderkamack Road
Oradell, N.J. 07649

Medical Tribune
110 East 59th Street
New York, N.Y. 10022

National Enquirer
600 S.E. Coast Avenue
Lantana, Fla. 33462

The New Yorker Magazine
25 West 43rd Street
New York, N.Y. 10036

Official Detective Stories
235 Park Avenue South
New York, N.Y. 10013

Parade
57 Lena Avenue
Freeport, N.Y. 11520

Progressive Farmer
Box 2581
Birmingham, Ala. 35202

Sports Afield
250 West 55th Street
New York, N.Y. 10019

Successful Farming
1716 Locust Street
Des Moines, Iowa 50336

True
1515 Broadway
New York, N.Y. 10036

World
488 Madison Avenue
New York, N.Y. 10022

ALPHABETICAL LIST
OF CARTOONISTS

ALPHABETICAL LIST OF COMIC STRIPS

ALPHABETICAL LIST
OF CARTOON CAPTIONS

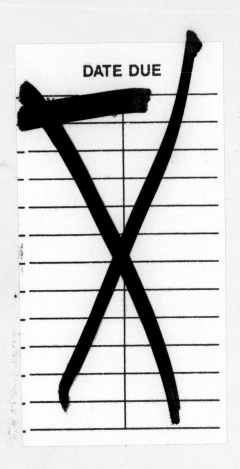